WITHDRAWN

W9-BTG-117

THE MODERN SPIRIT

BOOKS BY ROBERT LANGBAUM

The Modern Spirit:
Essays on the Continuity of Nineteenth- and Twentieth-Century
Literature

The Poetry of Experience:
The Dramatic Monologue in Modern Literary Tradition

The Gayety of Vision:
A Study of Isak Dinesen's Art

AS EDITOR

Shakespeare's *The Tempest*

The Victorian Age:
Essays in History and in Social and Literary Criticism

THE MODERN SPIRIT

Essays on the Continuity of Nineteenth-
and Twentieth-Century Literature

ROBERT LANGBAUM

CUMBERLAND COUNTY COLLEGE
LIBRARY P.O. BOX 517 VINELAND N.J.

New York OXFORD UNIVERSITY PRESS 1970

PR
99
L32

70-665

Copyright © 1959, 1964, 1965, 1966, 1967, 1968, 1970 by Robert Langbaum
Library of Congress Catalogue Card Number: 70-83012
Printed in the United States of America

To my daughter
Donata Emily

PREFACE

With one exception, the essays in this volume were published or
delivered orally during the last five years. The dates and places of
original publication or oral delivery are listed in the Acknowledg-
ments. Since the subjects and occasions of the individual essays
are diverse, this book makes no claim to unity. Yet the reader will,
I hope, find that the essays when read together ring changes upon
a number of recurring themes—themes that reflect my own continuing concern with the question of modernism, of what consti-
tutes the modern spirit in literature and life. My main purpose in
collecting these essays is not to draw out the recurring themes—it
is the essays themselves that matter—but I hope that the essays
will gain in richness through the reverberations among them and
through the implicit accrual, as the reader moves forward, of an
idea of the modern.

By modern, I mean the post-Enlightenment tradition that connects the nineteenth and twentieth centuries. This will be evident
enough if I name just a few of the themes that recur here—the
new nineteenth-century concept of culture, for example, or the

nineteenth-century concept of history as involving development or evolutionary process. Both concepts continue into our own time. But the continuity traced here is dynamic. And we see, as we move from the nineteenth to the twentieth century, changing ideas about nature, a continuing but changing interest in questions of self and identity, and a developing interest, that becomes evident in the twentieth century, in the cyclical view of history, and in myth and the tragicomic attitude that accompanies the mythical view of life.

I hope that by the time the reader comes to the end he will understand why I have chosen to conclude a volume such as this with an essay on Shakespeare's *The Tempest*. On the one hand, *The Tempest*, in its idea of order and treatment of nature, makes a nice Renaissance contrast to the modern. On the other hand, the special twentieth-century taste for *The Tempest*, and for Shakespeare's last plays generally, demonstrates that interest in the mythical and tragicomic view of life which is discussed in preceding essays on Browning, E.M. Forster and Yeats.

These essays have been revised in varying degrees, but none radically. Notes have been added at the back for those readers who may find it useful to refer to them. I want to thank the editors and publishers who allowed me to reprint the essays. I want also to thank those friends who took time to read parts of this book and offer valuable suggestions: Jacques Barzun, E.D. Hirsch, Jr., Cecil Lang, M.L. Rosenthal, Anthony Winner. Thanks, too, to John B. Cobb, Jr., Irvin Ehrenpreis, Arthur Kirsch and Calvin Woodard, who answered questions. I am grateful to Marianne Moore who, when I first wrote about her poems, graciously consented to answer a few questions about them. I am grateful to the Wordsworth Library, Dove Cottage, Grasmere, which made available to me their priceless collection of Wordsworth manuscripts. Thanks finally to the University of Virginia's Alderman Library and to the University's Research Grants Committee which helped with clerical expenses.

Charlottesville, Va.   R. L.
February 1970

ACKNOWLEDGMENTS

Earlier versions of the essays in this volume have appeared elsewhere:

"The Function of Criticism Once More," in *The Yale Review*, 54:2 (Winter 1965), 205–218.

"The Evolution of Soul in Wordsworth's Poetry," in *PMLA*, 82:2 (May 1967), 265–272, copyright 1967 by the Modern Language Association of America. Reprinted by permission of the Modern Language Association of America.

"The Victorian Idea of Culture," as Introduction to *The Victorian Age: Essays in History and in Social and Literary Criticism*, edited by Robert Langbaum, Second Edition, Revised, copyright © 1967 by Fawcett Publications, Inc. Reprinted by permission of Fawcett Publications, Inc.

"The Dynamic Unity of *In Memoriam*," read under a different title on March 8, 1969, at the 125th Anniversary of Saint Mary's College, Notre Dame, Indiana.

"Browning and the Question of Myth," in *PMLA*, 81:7 (December 1966), 575–584, copyright 1966 by the Modern Language Association of America. Reprinted by permission of the Modern Language Association of America.

"The New Nature Poetry," in *The American Scholar*, 28:3 (Summer 1959), 323–340.

"A New Look at E. M. Forster," in *The Southern Review*, 4:1 (Winter 1968), 33–49.

"Mailer's New Style," in *Novel*, 2:1 (Fall 1968), 69–78.

"The Mysteries of Identity: A Theme in Modern Literature," in *The American Scholar*, 34:4 (Autumn 1965), 569–586.

"*The Tempest* and Tragicomic Vision," as Introduction to *The Tempest* by William Shakespeare, edited by Robert Langbaum, copyright © 1964 by Robert Langbaum. Reprinted by permission of The New American Library, Inc., New York.

Thanks are due to the following publishers: Merle Armitage for permission to quote from Don Gifford's translation of Kleist's "Marionette Theatre," in Armitage's edition of *Five Essays on Klee*, Duell, Sloane and Pearce. Doubleday and Company, with Faber and Faber Ltd., for permission to quote from "Meditation at Oyster River" by Theodore Roethke in *The Collected Poems of Theodore Roethke*, copyright © by Beatrice Roethke as Administratrix to the Estate. Harcourt, Brace and World, with Faber and Faber Ltd., for permission to quote from Richard Wilbur's "The Death of a Toad" in *Ceremony and Other Poems* (New York), *Poems 1943–1956* (London). Harper and Row, with Faber and Faber Ltd., for permission to quote from Ted Hughes's "Pike" in *Lupercal* and "Ghost Crabs" in *Wodwo*. Holt, Rinehart and Winston, with Jonathan Cape Ltd., for permission to quote from "Stopping by Woods," "The Need of Being Versed in Country Things," "Come In," "In Hardwood Groves," "An Old Man's Winter Night," "After Apple Picking," "Design," "Desert Places," and "Build Soil," in *Complete Poems of Robert Frost*, copyright 1916, 1923, 1930, 1934, 1939 by Holt, Rinehart and Winston, Inc., copyright 1936, 1942, 1944, 1951, © 1958, 1962 by Robert Frost, copyright © 1964, 1967 by Lesley Frost Ballantine. Alfred A. Knopf and Random House, with Martin Secker and Warburg Ltd., for permission to quote from Thomas Mann's copyrighted

Essays of Three Decades and *Joseph and His Brothers*, both translated by H.T. Lowe-Porter; with Granada Publishing Ltd., for permission to quote from W.S. Merwin's copyrighted *Green with Beasts*; with Faber and Faber Ltd., for permission to quote from copyrighted *The Collected Poems of Wallace Stevens*; and with Chatto and Windus Ltd., for permission to use a passage from my copyrighted book, *The Gayety of Vision: A Study of Isak Dinesen's Art.* The Macmillan Company, with Faber and Faber Ltd., for permission to quote from "A Grave," "The Plumet Basilisk," "The Fish," and "The Jerboa," in Marianne Moore's *Collected Poems*, copyright 1935 by Marianne Moore, renewed 1963 by Marianne Moore and T. S. Eliot, and from "The Steeple-Jack," in *Collected Poems*, copyright 1951 by Marianne Moore; and with M. B. Yeats and Macmillan Ltd., for permission to quote from "Beautiful Lofty Things," "Municipal Gallery Revisited," "A Bronze Head," and "Lapis Lazuli," in W. B. Yeats's *Collected Poems*, copyright 1940 by Georgie Yeats, renewed 1968 by Bertha Georgie Yeats, Michael Butler Yeats, Anne Yeats, and from "Among School Children," in *Collected Poems*, copyright 1928 by The Macmillan Company, renewed 1968 by Georgie Yeats. Oxford University Press, with Chatto and Windus Ltd., for permission to quote from Richard Eberhart's "The Groundhog," in *Collected Poems 1930–1960*, © 1960 by Richard Eberhart. New Directions Publishing Corporation, with J.M. Dent and Sons Ltd. and the Trustees for the Copyrights of the late Dylan Thomas, for permission to quote from "A Refusal to Mourn," in *The Collected Poems of Dylan Thomas*, copyright 1939 by New Directions Publishing Corporation, copyright 1952 by Dylan Thomas. The Viking Press, with Laurence Pollinger Ltd., and the Estate of the late Mrs. Frieda Lawrence, for permission to quote from "Fish" by D. H. Lawrence, in *The Complete Poems of D. H. Lawrence*, Vol. I, edited by Vivian de Sola Pinto and F. Warren Roberts, copyright 1923, renewed 1951 by Frieda Lawrence, and from 5 June 1914 letter to Garnett, in *The Collected Letters of D. H. Lawrence*, edited by Harry T. Moore, copyright 1932 by The Estate of D. H. Lawrence, copyright © renewed 1960 by Angelo Ravagli and C. Montague Weekley, Executors of the Estate of Frieda Lawrence Ravagli, all rights reserved.

CONTENTS

THE MODERN SPIRIT

THE
FUNCTION
OF CRITICISM
ONCE MORE

I allude in my title to Matthew Arnold's most famous essay, because I want to start by suggesting that the literary situation Arnold called for in Victorian England has largely come to pass in both England and America in our time. That is our problem. In "The Function of Criticism at the Present Time," Arnold complained that the English of his day were indifferent to criticism and that this was why England had not produced an adequate modern literature. In modern times, at least, Arnold said, an intense critical effort is necessary to prepare the cultural climate out of which a great literature can be produced. And he suggested that it would be necessary in the immediate future to pour more energy into the writing of criticism than into the writing of poetry.

Now since the Second World War, we have been hearing a complaint which is just the opposite of Arnold's. This is, we are told on every side, an age of criticism; and we are usually told this by people who do not like critics or criticism. Unlike Arnold, these people say that there is too much criticism, and that *that* is what's wrong with poetry. In 1954, Malcolm Cowley, in a book called

3

The Literary Situation, called this a new Alexandrian age in which the creative writer has been displaced by the rhetorician. And shortly thereafter, the poet, Karl Shapiro, published a book, called appropriately *In Defense of Ignorance,* in which he blamed the critics for just about everything, but especially for getting in the way between the poet and his audience—an audience which left to itself would love and understand poetry. Both in politics and literature, the advanced young people of the 1960's have turned against the critical spirit of the fifties, so that Susan Sontag, for example, defiantly entitles her 1966 collection of critical essays, *Against Interpretation.* The critic is the scapegoat of the literary scene— blamed by the public for the bad state of literature, blamed by the writers for the bad state of the public.

In answer to Cowley, I would like to say that the present situation is unlike the Alexandrian in that the brilliant period of modern criticism beginning with Eliot and I. A. Richards in the early twenties does not follow but coincides with the brilliant period of modern creative writing, and has been mainly concerned to support that writing. Miss Sontag, too, turns out to be arguing against a kind of criticism that is not most characteristically modern—the kind that explains content or meaning. As for Karl Shapiro's naïve faith in the possibilities of communication, anyone who has read Richards's *Practical Criticism* will have seen how appalling were the untutored reactions to poetry of Richards's students, who were among the best of the Cambridge undergraduates. But then anyone who has tried teaching poetry to undergraduates, or has himself had the experience of *learning* to understand and love a work of art, which may at first have seemed repellent, will have his own answer to Shapiro.

Critics of course have always been attacked, and not only by disappointed authors. We all resent them to some degree as the censors or superegos of the literary process—the enemies to spontaneity, creativity, life. Yet it is generally agreed that criticism is an issue in our day as it never has been before, and that modern criticism is in some way different from the criticism that has gone before.

What then is the difference? There are two ways of answering that question. We can take the easy way and say that the critics must live, that the bright young assistant professors must have their promotions. Certainly, the enormous expansion of the universities and of the funds available for research have enabled, and indeed encouraged, more men than ever before to devote themselves to criticism. But that doesn't explain why so many men of the highest energy and intelligence, men who might have achieved distinction in any number of careers, should have chosen to devote themselves to criticism. It is easy enough to understand why a man who has the gift should want to write poems or novels. But to write books about other men's books? This is hard to understand. Indeed, when one sees the army of intelligent men who nowadays devote whole careers to the explications of texts, the counting up of images, the tracking down of sources, and so on, one is tempted to exclaim that nothing short of the Bible could be worth that much attention.

But then one realizes that modern criticism really rests on the assumption—an assumption not fully brought to consciousness in many critics—that literature is a kind of continuing bible, that it is the only continuing source of revelation, the only value-making, as opposed to value remembering or value-describing, force in the modern world. Aristotle, in answer to Plato's attack on poetry in *The Republic*, established poetry as a mode of knowledge—knowledge of the order *in* nature. But modern criticism goes farther. It treats poetry as the creator of the very order to be known, as the only creator of values in a world where the other branches of knowledge have either ceased to deal with values or have limited themselves to analyzing and describing values.

There is of course nothing new in the idea that great works of literature are bibles. Blake said so, and so, in less explicit ways, did the other romanticists. Coleridge, the greatest of the English ro-

mantic critics, is the father of the modern criticism I am talking
about, because he articulated most completely the romantic theory
of the imagination—the theory of the imagination as the creative
faculty, the faculty by which man brings something new into the
world, something which was never there before. The theory of the
imagination was conceived as an answer to the seventeenth- and
eighteenth-century scientific view of man as entirely a product of
his physical environment, as having nothing psychical inside him
that had not come from outside. Science had rationalized the soul
out of man, and the romanticists restored it by way of the secular
concept of imagination. The imagination was for the romanticists,
and it remains for us, the faculty which accounts for literature as
revelation, as a maker of values.

It is interesting to note how the problem faced by the romanticists in regard to the seventeenth-century psychology of Locke has
come up again in our time in regard to computers. In talking to
scientists who work with computers, I have been amazed at how
frightened they are of them and how in their conversation they
tend to personify and even deify computers. This surprises me because having been given some idea of the way in which computers
are "programmed," I find myself far more impressed by the inge-
nuity of the programmers than by the computers. I have come to
realize that the reason the computer men are so frightened of
their Frankensteins is not that they don't know all about
computers—of course they do; it is that they don't know enough
about the human mind. They take too simple, too mechanical a
view of it. And at the mechanical function, the computer will beat
us every time.

Now Lockean man was like a computer in that he gave out only
what had been "programmed" into him. The romanticists' answer
was that he didn't exist, because man has a faculty, called imagination, which reaches out and creates the world it perceives. Every
fact is a creation with a piece of mind, and therefore with value or
significance, in it. (I have liked pointing out to the computer men

that what they feed into their machines are created facts and not the raw flux of experience.) The main evidence for the romanticists that there is such a faculty as imagination, that man does put out things that cannot entirely be accounted for by what he has taken in—the main evidence was art. And sure enough, in all the fearful discussions about computers, the question that inevitably comes up is: will we ever be able to make computers that will paint great pictures or write great poems? In the modern world, art remains as the last great sign of man's freedom or indeterminacy. And I cite this highly topical instance to show that if the idea of literature as revelation bears so closely upon the pressing question of computers, then it is not so difficult to understand why it is worthwhile to be a critic—to be one of the people who help explain what it is that is being revealed and what its implications are.

As a sign of how far the concept of literature as revelation has gone since Coleridge, I need only allude to the most ambitious work of criticism of recent years—Northrop Frye's *Anatomy of Criticism*. Frye sees the forms—the images, that is, and myths—which the imagination projects into the world as giving value-making coherence not only to literature but to all verbal structures. Is it not true, he suggests at the end of his book, "that the verbal structures of psychology, anthropology, theology, history, law, and everything else built out of words have been informed or constructed by the same kind of myths or metaphors that we find, in their original hypothetical form, in literature?" Myths are, in other words, the mathematical equations of all possible verbal structures. Therefore the critic, says Frye—in a closing statement which should bring in many new candidates for so high an office—the critic, he says, holds the "keys to dreamland." This means that the critic holds the master key to all forms of verbal discourse, and is in a position to reforge "the broken links between creation and knowledge, art and science, myth and concept. . . . This will appear to be, with increasing obviousness," Frye says, "the social and practical result of their [the critics'] labors." [1] Frye has completely articulated the ultimate aim of Coleridge's vast and notoriously unfinished efforts. He has been able to describe even more completely than Arnold what in modern times the social function of criticism ought to be. For he has had at his disposal more psychology and anthropology and more comparative mythology than Arnold. He has also had in the work of Yeats, Joyce and Eliot the example of that more adequate modern literature that Arnold was calling for.

I have often thought that the climate of ideas shared by these three twentieth-century writers—the climate made by Frazer, by Freud and Jung, by the dissemination of Hegel through Marx, and by the rediscovery of Vico—I have often thought that this climate of ideas was after all the fulfillment of the thing Arnold wanted criticism to provide. Arnold never intended that the ideas should be strictly literary ideas—I don't think there are such things anyway. Nor did he ever think of criticism as a strictly literary activity.

This brings me around to my next question, which is this. If Frye is completing the thought of Coleridge and Arnold, then what is new about modern criticism? Mainly, I would say, the large body of nonliterary concepts by which the modern critic is able to justify, elaborate and apply the romantic intuitions about the existence of the imagination and about the truth of what the imagination perceives. The most important of these concepts derive from three areas of nonliterary thought. One, the dialectical view of history as expounded by Hegel and Marx, the view that mind evolves historically and that reality evolves with it, since each age makes its own imaginative construct of reality, has its own world-view, each true in the way that imaginative constructs are true. As one of the most genuine expressions of these world-views, literature becomes a book of historical revelation, which for Hegelians and Marxists would be ultimate revelation.

Two, the comparative study of mythology, in such works as Frazer's *Golden Bough*. By revealing a common pattern in various mythologies, these studies suggest that all myths are true in the way imaginative constructs are true, and that they speak their own profound language. Thus, the modern critic is able to justify the romantic taste for the marvelous and the conviction of the romanticists that there was something profound in the marvelous, though they could not always say what it was.

Third, and by far the most important, Freud's not so much discovery as naming and analysis of the subconscious. By making the subconscious an operational concept, Freud justifies the romantic conviction that the rationalists had left man only a portion of his mind. Imagination was the name the romanticists gave to the whole mind of man in operation. Romantic poetry might be said to specialize in giving us, through suggestive resonances, a sense of the hidden area of the mind; but the nineteenth-century critics had not the vocabulary to say much about that hidden area. They could respond sensitively to its presence in works of all periods, and talk about their response. They could practice, in other words —as did Coleridge and Hazlitt in evoking the inner life of Shakespeare's characters, or Ruskin in rendering verbally the effect of pictorial art, as Arnold did with his famous "touchstones," and Pater after him—they could practice impressionistic criticism.

Impressionistic criticism has a very bad name nowadays. It is the technique the modern critics have reacted most violently against.[2] Yet impressionism was the only way to get at the subconscious resonances of a poem, until Freud gave critics the concepts by which to analyze the thing they were sensing. Freud not only gave a name to the hidden area of the mind, but explained its workings in detail. His studies of errors, of wit, of dreams, all suggested that there was a special 'logic' of the subconscious, which looked to critics very like the 'logic' of the imagination and of art. Here was a gold mine to be exploited—a way to talk about the literary work itself, not the biography of the author, or the history of the times, but the very work itself, and in talking about it to be able to think with all the depth, swiftness, subtlety, suppleness and complexity of art itself—far beyond the possibilities of ordinary discursive thought. Some of the liveliest minds in England and America jumped in to exploit that mine, and they gave us perhaps the liveliest period of criticism we have yet had. By the time people began complaining about the age of criticism, a few years after the end of the Second World War, the mine seemed to have been used up. It looked as though the best modern criticism had been written.

To get back to our question: what then is new about modern criticism? Modern criticism may be defined as that criticism which found itself in a position to take up where Coleridge left off. The exploitation of the new nonliterary concepts accounts for what we have considered to be the two main schools of modern criticism— that which works from outside in on a literary work, and that which works from inside out. I define both schools by the same definition to suggest that there never were two schools, that the second, the so-called New Criticism, was a local divergence from the main stream, and that they are both parts of the main stream of moral, psychological and social criticism that goes back through Arnold to Coleridge, and from Coleridge through the great classical critics to Aristotle.

It is the New Critics who are usually meant when modern criticism is attacked. The New Critics are attacked because they seem to stress words over ideas. They point out that the paraphrasable prose meaning of a poem is often the least interesting thing about it ("Gather ye rosebuds while ye may," for example, or "How time has changed me"), but that the real meaning of a poem is in the action of its words upon each other. They point to the kind of poem that takes two opposite stands at the same time, thus negating the possibility of *meaning* in a prose sense in order that it may *mean* in a poetic sense. All this, to people interested in the human.

element in poetry, sounds very academic, very anti-life. But what the New Critics are saying is that poetry is about a complex state of consciousness of which ideas are only one, very inadequate expression.

Their view of language, developed by Richards, is also *psychological* rather than logical, in that they consider that words have in their contexts—their contexts in individual and collective experience—an organic life like that of consciousness. Of this organic life, any specific meaning of the word is, like meaning in poetry, only one inadequate expression. Poetic discourse uses more of the organic life of the word than prose discourse does.

I am not going to defend the New Criticism because as a movement it is, I am convinced, dead—dead of its very success. We are all New Critics nowadays, whether we like it or not, in that we cannot avoid discerning and appreciating wit in poetry, or reading with close attention to words, images, ironies and so on. "'The term 'The New Criticism,'" as T. S. Eliot has pointed out in his essay "The Frontiers of Criticism," refers to such a wide variety of critics that its currency would seem simply to be a recognition "that the more distinguished critics of to-day, however widely they differ from each other, all differ in some significant way from the critics of a previous generation." [3] One sees now that the New Criticism was a necessary divergence from the main stream of criticism, a necessary time out for retooling. It was new precisely because it was making the tools necessary to exploit for literature the new gold mine of nonliterary concepts. Now that the New Criticism has done its work, we can return with these tools to the main stream of criticism.

Before I go on to this main stream, I would like to indicate the connection between the New Critical tools and the new nonliterary concepts I have been talking about. The New Critics take off from the idea—which is the fruit of all these nonliterary concepts —that there is a special 'logic' of the imagination. They go on to show that there is consequently a special language of poetry distinct from, but for its purposes just as exact as, the language of discursive prose. The New Critics have done their best work with poetry, and they have done more than any critics since Coleridge to re-establish, after the challenge of science, the intellectual validity of poetry, to rescue poetry from the general modern sense of it as a kind of inexact prose decorated with metaphors and 'souped up' with emotion.

Now the New Critics' case for the exactness of poetic language rests on the new nonliterary concepts, especially psychological concepts and especially—as the movement developed from Richards to Empson to such American New Critics as Ransom, Tate, Brooks, Warren—Freudian concepts. The idea of subconscious processes leads to the idea of other dimensions of reality. Images or symbols are pre-conscious and pre-analytic modes of thinking. When used consciously in poetry, they are, far from being mere decoration, the most exact modes for thinking with both the conscious and unconscious mind about the whole of reality.

Most of the favorite New Critical terms and ideas can, I think, be accounted for by this connection of poetry with the subconscious. Ambiguities of meaning and ambivalences of judgment are, for example, good things, because all possible meanings of a word operate at the same time in dream or free association, where connotation is usually more important than denotation. And as for ambivalence, one object can in a dream symbolize opposite things; subconsciously, we can both love and hate the same person. Freud has shown the psychological 'logic' by which such anomalies can be understood and this psychological 'logic' is analogous to the 'logic' of art, to the orchestration of meanings by which certain art communicates.

Even the so-called anti-romantic revolution against the resonating, suggestive style of nineteenth-century poetry, and in favor of a witty, a metaphysical poetry—even this so-called classical revolution in taste is, I think, connected with the new interest in the subconscious. For the kind of wit the New Critics like is just the kind Pope and Dr. Johnson did not like. The New Critics like the psychological wit of Donne, the kind of wit so brilliantly analyzed by Coleridge when he pointed out that Hamlet is most witty when he is most disturbed emotionally. Dr. Johnson's pejorative description of metaphysical wit, as a yoking together of the most heterogeneous ideas, resembles Coleridge's description of the synthesizing power of the imagination. The New Critics like, in other words, the kind of wit which is not merely a rhetorical device but which is an equivalent for emotion—which is, as Freud showed in his study of wit, rooted in subconscious processes.

To sum up, then, the contribution of the New Criticism. If we start with the idea that there is a special 'logic' of the imagination and that poetry is a serious body of knowledge, even of revelation, then it behooves us to find out and to be able to talk about what the poem itself is saying. For what it is saying will be more complex than anything you could learn about it through a study of its sources, or of the period in which it was written, or of the author's life and ideas. The sort of procedure from which it has delivered us is that of the old-time English professor who, in teaching Marvell's "Coy Mistress," would talk about the English Civil War and about Marvell's life, his Puritanism, his reading, his friendship with Milton, and finally, just as the bell rang, would say, "And as for the poem, gentlemen, beautiful, beautiful." The story explains why the New Critics had to adopt that particular strategy of combat.

What then are the limitations of the New Criticism? It has been insufficiently critical of itself. Although this is changing, the New Critics have not until recently seemed sufficiently aware that their method would work better for some kinds of literature than for others, and that it would work for some kinds not at all. Nor have they shown a sense of how much of their method could be applied where. Their method works best for a highly intense lyric poetry, and well, though less well, for the kind of fiction and drama that share the characteristics of a highly intense lyric poetry (less well because fiction and drama do not so easily lend themselves to microscopic analysis). Their method works best for modern, metaphysical, and—oddly enough, since they are supposed to be so down on it—romantic poetry; they have done some of their best work on romantic poems. The fact is that the New Criticism works best, is indeed necessary, for the literature that deals with the subconscious and with a multi-dimensional reality, but deals with them as psychological experience, and not—like Dante or Spenser—as allegory. This may be because the allegorical poet has himself done the critic's work of analysis and given us the result.

The main limitation of the New Criticism, however, is that it has been an incomplete criticism. That is why it has been insufficiently aware of the specifically modern grounds of its own methods and taste, and insufficiently aware of its own connection with the main stream of criticism. The New Critics have confined their aim to understanding the text—which was, as I have indicated, a necessary strategy. Understanding the text is a matter of technique, and the New Critics have liked to think of themselves as technicians. But the technician must always in the end put his tools at the service of the man who knows what he wants to use them for. And understanding the text, if we may judge by the best criticism of the past, is where criticism begins, not where it ends.

That brings me around to what I consider to be the main stream of modern criticism. It is defined rather more by ends than methods. In the open acknowledgment of our ends, of what we are at least potentially trying to do, lies I think the answer to the questions raised by our age of criticism. T. S. Eliot, who is often held responsible for having got all this burst of critical activity started, asked the crucial question about it in the 1956 essay I have already quoted, "The Frontiers of Criticism." After acknowledging the unprecedentedly large scope of modern criticism, which traces its descent from Coleridge just because it was Coleridge who first introduced into literary criticism the outside disciplines of philosophy, aesthetics and psychology: after acknowledging all this, Eliot goes on to wonder whether the "very richness and variety" of modern criticism has not obscured its ultimate purpose. "I wonder," he says, "whether the weakness of modern criticism is not an uncertainty as to what criticism is for? As to what benefit it is to bring, and to whom? . . . Every critic may have his eye on a definite goal, may be engaged on a task which needs no justification, and yet criticism itself may be lost as to its aims."

That is a very good statement of the problem. On the solution, however, I part company with Mr. Eliot. For his answer is to define the *limits* of literary criticism—he uses *frontiers* in the European sense of limits, whereas I would use the word in President Kennedy's American sense. Eliot would keep literary criticism from passing over into something else—into biography and source-hunting on the one side, which does not, he says, promote the understanding of poetry as poetry, and into excessive analysis or "lemon-squeezing" on the other, which does not promote its enjoyment. When Eliot says that biographical information is relevant to our understanding of Wordsworth but not to our understanding of his poetry, I feel we no longer need that kind of strategy, that we can now afford to admit that our understanding of Wordsworth is bound to have some bearing on our understanding of his poetry. And when Eliot speaks disparagingly of people who want poetry to be "explained to them in terms of something else," [4] I ask how anything can be explained except in terms of something else. I don't know whether there is such a thing as pure poetry, but I am sure there is no such thing as pure criticism. For the critic's job is to translate from one mode of discourse to another. His job is to analyze, and you analyze by applying concepts to an object.

Fortunately for us, Eliot has not himself stayed within the limits he prescribes for literary criticism. His criticism has been connected with a social and religious position. He has written on all these matters and shown their connections. Yeats's criticism is part of an even more elaborately worked-out metaphysical, historical and political position. Whether they intended to follow Arnold or not, Yeats and Eliot are just the sort of critics Arnold had in mind —critics who have brought together ideas from the past and the present and from diverse cultures in such a way as to show us our connection and disconnection with the past and the price at which cultural unity might be achieved in our time. Since Aristotle, the greatest critics have been those whose criticism has been part of an articulated world-view. It is this sort of criticism that is in the main stream. The modern critics who have consciously followed Arnold—Eliot himself, for all his protest against Arnold; also Edmund Wilson, F. R. Leavis, Lionel Trilling—have been consciously in the main stream. The others have been in it to the extent that they contributed to a complete criticism.

When I speak of a complete criticism, I do not mean that each critic must do the whole job himself. Each critic ought, however, to understand what criticism as a whole is doing, so he can know where his own work fits in. Let me sketch out briefly the sort of thing a complete criticism might do. In addition to explaining texts, a complete criticism would go on to explore the questions that inevitably occur to the serious reader who has understood a text. Such a reader wants to know how this particular work relates to and modifies the literary tradition, and how it relates to and modifies other branches of knowledge. He wants to understand the relevance of the work to its time and to him and his time, the reasons he likes or dislikes the work, and what his liking or disliking tells him about himself and his time. The *modern* reader wants to place both himself and the work historically, and to determine, as a consequence, what the implications of the work are for his politics, his religion and his life style—for such questions as whether he ought to be a proper citizen or a bohemian, how he ought to raise his children, whether he ought to live in the city or the country (nobody ever recommends the suburbs). He will also want to read back from his cultural situation to the work to ask whether, fine as the work is, or important as it was in its time, it has anything to say to him now; and he may have to wait for some critic to discover for him—by reseeing the work through new concepts, a new vocabulary—its modern relevance. Modern relevance does not necessarily mean finding modern topics or attitudes. It might mean a certain relevant otherness that helps us by contrast to define our own modernity. The relevance of Dante is an example.

A complete criticism, I would say, completes the literary process by dealing not only with the text, the part of the literary process over which the author has control, but also by dealing with that part of the literary process over which the author has little control —the part that takes place before the author begins to write and after he finishes, the part that takes place before the reader opens the book and after he closes it. It is legitimate, for example, to use literature as a source for studying the nature of the creative process and thus of the mind. A complete criticism takes care of that part of the literary process which the author cannot take care of himself. The complete critic must, like the creative writer, know not only literature but life.

If the work of art is, as so many modern critics like to tell us, a self-contained entity, a revelation, a private affair between writer and reader—and this is truer of some works than of others—then the critic's job is to turn the work of art into something that can be thought about and talked about. His job is to do, in the most intelligent, learned and disciplined manner possible, the thing that must happen in any case just to the extent that the work lingers in our minds after we have closed the book. His job is to turn the work of art into a cultural acquisition. This has always been, and it remains, the function of criticism, and it is to the continuance of this function that the *newest* critics will undoubtedly bring all their latest techniques. In performing this function, the newest critics will show that, apart from its service to literature, criticism has in modern times a special importance of its own as, in an increasingly technological age, the application to all the affairs of life of what we may call the literary or humanistic, in contrast with the technical, mind.

THE EVOLUTION
OF SOUL
IN WORDSWORTH'S
POETRY

When Keats in a letter calls this world "The vale of Soul-making,"
he comes close to Wordsworth's way of thinking.[1] For Keats says
that we come into the world as pure potentiality or "Intelligence"
and that we acquire a "Soul" or "sense of Identity" through
"Circumstances." And it is the main purport of Wordsworth's
poetry to show the spiritual significance of this world, to show that
we evolve a soul or identity through experience and that the very
process of evolution is what we mean by *soul*.

To understand the implications of Wordsworth's view and why
it is distinctively modern, we have to go back to the psychological
assertions that Wordsworth was both absorbing and answering—
we have to go back to Locke and Locke's disciple Hartley.[2] The
best analogy to the challenge raised by Locke is the challenge
raised in our time by computers. For Lockean man is like a computer in that everything inside him comes from outside, through
sensation; so that Lockean man gives back only what has been
"programmed" into him. Even his choices are no evidence of free
will; for once the idea of choice has entered his head, he must

choose and he must choose between predetermined alternatives. "A man that is walking," says Locke, "to whom it is proposed to give off walking, is not at liberty, whether he will determine himself to walk, or give off walking or not: he must necessarily prefer one or the other of them; walking or not walking." [3] One would use the same line of reasoning to show that a computer, for all its ability to make choices, is not free.

Although Locke lays great emphasis on self-consciousness, in that he shows that the greatest part of mental life consists of reflections on our own ideas, his system does not, as Blake pointed out in "There is No Natural Religion," allow for anything new to come into the world, since Locke's "complex ideas" merely complicate a fixed number of sensations.[4] Lockean self-consciousness is the sort we may well predict for the formidable computers of the future.

As computers become increasingly complex, as they become capable of making choices, learning, and giving orders, we inevitably wonder at what point of complexity they can be considered human, as having a soul. Now in *The Prelude* Wordsworth was trying to answer some such question as this regarding Lockean man. If we consider that the human psyche is built up of sensations, then at what point do sensations add up to soul, or how do we jump from sensations to soul? We can understand Wordsworth's answer to Locke if we imagine him answering the question in regard to computers. His answer would be that computers will never be human until they are born and grow up.

If sensations turn into soul—into an ineffable quality that can never be accounted for by the sensations themselves—it is because the sensations reach an ever-changing mind that transforms them, as a merely passive receiver, the sort of mind Locke likens to blank paper, could not. No two succeeding sensations from the same object can be the same, because the later sensation reaches a mind already modified by the earlier sensation. Locke recognizes all this, but it remains for Wordsworth to draw the necessary conclusions in his poetry and for Coleridge to formulate them in his theory of the imagination. The necessary conclusions are summed up in the idea of interchange between man and nature—the idea that the mind modifies sensation as much as sensation modifies the mind.

It may be argued that computers, too, as they learn, offer a changing receiver to external data. This brings us to the second important point in Wordsworth's answer to Locke. Wordsworth portrays the mind as itself part of the nature it perceives; and it is this connection, sensed through what Wordsworth calls *joy*, that gives us confidence in the reality of ourselves and the external world. Dare one predict that no computer is likely to have this organic connection or to sense it through *joy*?

In *The Prelude*, Wordsworth tells us that his life began to the sound of the Derwent River that "loved / To blend his murmurs with my nurse's song" and "sent a voice / That flowed along my dreams," making

> ceaseless music that composed my thoughts
> To more than infant softness, giving me
> Amid the fretful dwellings of mankind
> A foretaste, a dim earnest, of the calm
> That Nature breathes among the hills and groves.
>   (1.270–281) [5]

There, in the best Lockean fashion, Wordsworth traces all his mature thoughts back to the sound of the river. But unlike Locke, Wordsworth presents the perceiving mind as active. The nurse's song with which the river blends is a sign that the mind is analogous to the river; that is why the river's voice flows along the dreams of the growing Wordsworth. When we read that the river "loved / To blend," we understand that the baby did not merely receive but loved the river's sound, reached out to it as a flower reaches out to the sun and air and rain it has the potentiality to receive. The blending and interchange turn sensation into experience, an experience of joy that will in future years spread around the mature man's thoughts an affective tone—a tone objectified in "the calm / That Nature breathes." This tone, this atmosphere of the mind, sensed as at once inside and outside the mind, is what the mature man will call *soul*.

The river received on its "smooth breast the shadow of those towers" of Cockermouth Castle (1.283). The reflection of the towers was perceived, we gather, at a somewhat later age than the sound of the river. Visual sensations are in Wordsworth more intellectual than sensations of sound. The composite experience of river and towers—which might be understood as an experience of female and male principles—stands behind the experiences of beauty and fear described in the rest of Book I, which are composite experiences of natural and moral power.

In Book II, the mature man's capacity for love is traced back to the contentment of the infant

> who sinks to sleep
> Rocked on his Mother's breast; who with his soul
> Drinks in the feelings of his Mother's eye!

Through his connection with his mother, he gains a sense of connection with nature, a connection portrayed through the imagery of flow and blending:

> No outcast he, bewildered and depressed:
> Along his infant veins are interfused
> The gravitation and the filial bond
> Of nature that connect him with the world.

The infant is from the start an active agent of perception who "drinks in" feelings. Because he inhabits the loving universe circumscribed for him by his mother's "Presence," he loves or reaches out to all that he beholds. That sense of "Presence," the baby's first apprehension of Deity, is produced by the sympathetic relation of mind to universe which is, says Wordsworth, the "Poetic spirit of our human life." The mind is portrayed as a relation and a process—a process *growing* from feeling through power, sense, thought, into the one great Mind and between subject and

object, in such a way that the parts flow one into the other and
can hardly be discriminated.

> For, feeling has to him imparted power
> That through the growing faculties of sense
> Doth like an agent of the one great Mind
> Create, creator and receiver both,
> Working but in alliance with the works
> Which it beholds.

This poetic spirit, says Wordsworth, is in most people "abated or
suppressed" in later years. But in some few it remains "Pre-emi-
nent till death," and those few are, we gather, poets (II.
235–265).

We have here an accounting for affect, for the value or "glory"
we find in the world, which seems to contradict the accounting in
the "Immortality Ode." The accounting in *The Prelude* is the authentically Wordsworthian one, because it is naturalistic, psychological and sensationalist. The Platonic idea of pre-existence is advanced in the "Ode"—Wordsworth tells us in the Fenwick note
to that poem—as a figure of speech, as a fanciful and traditional
way of generalizing the psychological phenomenon revealed to him
by his own life—that "the Child is Father of the Man," that spirit
is to be found in the primitive. "I took hold of the notion of pre-
existence," says Wordsworth, "as having sufficient foundation in
humanity for authorizing me to make for my purpose the best use
of it I could as a Poet." The Platonic idea is used with fine artistry
in the "Ode" as a counterpoint to the primitivist idea. It is the
primitivist idea that takes over when in stanza ix Wordsworth gets
down to the serious business of answering the question of the
poem, the question posed by the adult's sense of loss. His answer
is that nothing is lost. Even if we no longer experience the "glory"
we experienced in childhood, "nature yet remembers." Our souls,
he concludes in a strikingly primitivist image, can in a moment
travel backward

> And see the Children sport upon the shore,
> And hear the mighty waters rolling evermore.

Yet the Platonic idea is not lost sight of even here. It is so blended with the primitivist idea that we can see that its function all along has been to ennoble and spiritualize the primitivist idea. Thus the sea is the physical sea where all life began; but the sea is also immortal, through its very age ageless and transcendent:

> Hence in a season of calm weather
> Though inland far we be,
> Our Souls have sight of that immortal sea
> Which brought us hither.

Growing-up has been mainly compared to a journey of the sun across the sky; now it is compared to a journey inland from the sea. Wordsworth explains the adult's sense of loss by telling us that we come down from the sky and up from the sea, and by blending the two directions to evoke an original spiritual source that is unlocatable.

The blending goes even farther in the imagery through which Wordsworth tells us that the adult responds to the objects before him because he sees them through the lens of his memory of childhood experiences. Those "first affections" and "shadowy recollections," he says,

> Are yet the fountain light of all our day,
> Are yet a master light of all our seeing.

There is an inextricable blending here of light and water, the ideal and the primitive, Platonic metaphysics and Lockean psychology.

We find the same blending in two adjacent passages of *The Prelude*, Book I. In the first, Wordsworth speaks of experiences that cannot be accounted for by the Lockean theory of memory and association he has been developing—experiences which would seem to require, to account for them, some Platonic theory of "first-born affinities" (1.555), of archetypes, of innate ideas. He had such an experience when gazing over an expanse of sea,

> Of shining water, gathering as it seem'd,
> Through every hair-breadth of that field of light,
> New pleasure—   (1.578–580)

new, because not deriving from association with earlier pleasures.
Wordsworth evokes the transcendent quality of the experience by
turning shining *water* into a *field* of light, by dissolving both water
and land into light. But in the next passage, he says that he loves
to travel backward down through the corridors of memory, from
forms down through sensations, to recover at the point where conscious memory fades out just such a vision of light:

> Those recollected hours that have the charm
> Of visionary things, those lovely forms
> And sweet sensations that throw back our life,
> And almost make remotest infancy
> A visible scene, on which the sun is shining.
>   (1.631–635)

We have only to recall Locke's description of the mind as a
dark closet penetrated by certain rays of light from the outside
world,[6] we have only to recall this comparison, which is even more
revealing of Locke's outlook than his better known comparison of
the mind to white or blank paper, to understand the sense in
which Wordsworth answers Locke. Yet it is Locke who supplies
the concepts of memory and association through which Wordsworth can give psychological substantiation to his experience of his
own mind as light or music. And it is important to note that the
mind recognizes itself in an external sensation, that Wordsworth
arrives at his concept of mind by tracing his life back to an original sensation—to "A visible scene, on which the sun is shining" or
to the sound of the Derwent River.

Much ink has been spilled over the question whether Wordsworth believed that his apprehension of spirit came from outside

or inside, whether he was a Lockean empiricist [7] or a Platonic believer in innate ideas. The answer is that Wordsworth, when he is writing his best poetry, uses both doctrines as possibilities, blending them in such a way as to evoke the mystery he is talking about —the mystery of life, vitality, organic connection. The case should teach us something about the proper relation of ideas to poetry. And, indeed, Wordsworth himself pronounces on the subject in his first essay "Upon Epitaphs," where he speaks of the antithetical ideas of two Greek philosophers about the value of body in relation to soul. In spite of their opposite ideas, says Wordsworth, modulating from talk of thought to talk of feelings, "Each of these Sages was in sympathy with the best feelings of our Nature; feelings which, though they seem opposite to each other, have another and a finer connexion than that of contrast.—It is a connexion formed through the subtle progress by which, both in the natural and the moral world, qualities pass insensibly into their contraries, and things revolve upon each other." [8]

The case also suggests why The Prelude, which Wordsworth wrote with his left hand or deepest artistic instinct while trying with his right hand or conscious will to write the long philosophical poem Coleridge had put him up to, why The Prelude is so much more successful than what we have of that long philosophical poem, The Recluse, of which The Excursion is Part Two. The Prelude is successful, and successful as an appropriately modern poem of ideas, just because Wordsworth did not consider that he was at that point writing a philosophical poem. In the passage I have quoted above, he is apologizing to Coleridge for not getting on with the philosophical poem but dwelling instead, out of "an infirmity of love" for them, on "days / Disowned by memory" (1.614–615)—by conscious memory, that is.

To understand what Wordsworth has achieved in The Prelude, we have only to read Coleridge's description, in his Table Talk for 21 July 1832, long after he himself had turned against Locke and Hartley, of the original plan of The Recluse.

The plan laid out, and, I believe, partly suggested by me, was, that Wordsworth should assume the station of a man in mental repose, one whose principles were made up, and so prepared to deliver upon authority a system of philosophy. He was to treat man as man,—a subject of eye, ear, touch, and taste, in contact with external nature, and informing the senses from the mind, and not compounding a mind out of the senses.

Aside from the fact that *The Prelude* portrays a mind in evolution not in repose, we precisely do not find there the doctrinaire anti-Lockean stand described by Coleridge.

Wordsworth no sooner tells us in *The Prelude*, Book I, how nature through "extrinsic passion" or association first peopled his "mind with forms sublime or fair," than he speaks of other pleasures

Which, if I err not, surely must belong
To those first-born affinities that fit
Our new existence to existing things,
And, in our dawn of being, constitute
The bond of union between life and joy.

(554–558)

Note the tentativeness of "if I err not," and how even innate affinities are traced back to a primitive origin which one may still understand to be natural. Such blending evokes "the bond of union between life and joy" that is Wordsworth's answer to the question at the heart of *The Prelude*, the question that no simply rational account of life can answer. I mean the question, why live at all, why bother to get up in the morning? As so often in Wordsworth's best lines, the answer is couched in words that are general, even vague. Yet the "Presence" evoked, to use that other vague but potent Wordsworthian word, is definite enough and is the only answer to the question, "Why live?" We can infer that "the bond of union between life and joy" is the thing that will always distinguish human beings from computers. We can also infer that the philosopher's question, "Why live?" can only be answered by the poet. For the answer is that we take pleasure in the world we behold because we are one with it. And it is only the poet who can make pleasure and oneness real for us by just such blending as Wordsworth employs.

F. R. Leavis and Donald Davie have shown, through an analysis of Wordsworth's syntax, how he gives us poetry by blurring the thought.[9] One can say even more specifically that Wordsworth gives us poetry by being both Lockean and anti-Lockean at the same time. For Wordsworth answers Locke by using the Lockean concepts of memory and association. It is only through memory, says Locke, that the mind has any effectiveness, and he equates the self with the sum of conscious memory ("whatever has the consciousness of present and past actions, is the same person to whom they both belong"). But Locke does not speak of memory as modifying the actions remembered; these actions remain fixed, like the data 'remembered' by a computer. It is in speaking of the accidental association of ideas that Locke recognizes a modifying and transforming process. Locke accounts for our irrational behavior and for affect—for what he calls our "sympathies and antipathies"—by the connection through "chance or custom" of ideas that have no correspondence in nature or logic. Through association, in other words, sensations and ideas are transformed into something other than they would be in themselves, with a value they would not have in themselves.

The difference between Locke and the romanticists is that Locke deplores the process of association as unamenable to reason; [10] whereas the romanticists glory in it because it shows the mind as creative and carries them over from sensation to value. It is significant that Wordsworth and Coleridge were especially interested in the eighteenth-century medical doctor, David Hartley, who builds his whole system on the theory of association that is in Locke only one proposition. From association, Hartley derives the affective responses of pleasure and pain which lead to Christian values and faith. Hartley must have seemed to Wordsworth and Coleridge to have transcendentalized Locke. In "Religious Musings," Coleridge hails Hartley as "of mortal kind / Wisest," because he is the first to establish value on a materialistic and therefore scientific basis— the "first who marked the ideal tribes / Up the fine fibres through the sentient brain" (368–370). Hartley comes close to calling this world a vale of soul-making when he says: "Some degree of spirituality is the necessary consequence of passing through life. The sensible pleasures and pains must be transferred by association more and more every day, upon things that afford neither sensible pleasure nor sensible pain in themselves, and so beget the intellectual pleasures and pains." [11] In other words, we grow spiritually by conferring spirituality upon the world. The issue between the Locke-Hartley doctrine and the Platonic doctrine of pre-existence is whether we gain or lose spirituality by living.

Nevertheless, Hartley's system remains mechanical because he does not recognize that the crucial element in Locke's theory of association is this—that only in speaking of association does Locke allow for any unconscious mental process. Wordsworth and Coleridge modify Hartley by dwelling on the unconscious aspects of the associative process. Thus Coleridge, in turning against Hartley, says that "association depends in a much greater degree on the recurrence of resembling states of Feeling, than on Trains of Idea," and that "Ideas never recall Ideas . . . any more than Leaves in a forest create each other's motion—The Breeze it is that runs thro' them . . . the Soul, the state of Feeling." [12] Wordsworth says much the same thing when, in The Prelude, Book ii, he describes the delayed effect of epiphanies:

> the soul,
> Remembering how she felt, but what she felt
> Remembering not, retains an obscure sense
> Of possible sublimity, whereto
> With growing faculties she doth aspire
> With faculties still growing, feeling still

> That whatsoever point they gain, they yet
> Have something to pursue.   (315–322)

Association takes place not through the ideas or manifest content of an experience but through the affective tone, which can then be communicated to experiences with quite different manifest contents. Wordsworth makes clear what is implied by Coleridge's "Breeze"—that this affective tone is a feeling of infinity which connects the individual mind with the Great Mind and cannot be entirely accounted for by present, or even recollected, experience.

For Locke, we apprehend infinity as an idea of quantity—the result of our understanding that we can count indefinitely and can indefinitely add line segments to a given line segment. The idea is inapplicable, in the same way, to quality: "nobody ever thinks of infinite sweetness, or infinite whiteness." For Wordsworth, instead, we apprehend infinity as a feeling having to do with quality and organic wholeness—we cannot add to an organism as to a line segment. For Locke, the idea of infinity follows from our experience. For Wordsworth, we not only bring the feeling of infinity to later experiences through associated memory of earlier experiences, but the feeling somehow both rises out of and is anterior to even our primal experiences.

The ambiguity is projected through the use of both memory and the fading-out of memory. Because the soul remembers not what but how she felt, we carry with us a feeling larger than anything we can remember of our primal experiences; and the soul grows, in this vale of soul-making, toward a feeling of wholeness that seems recollected though we cannot say from where. Locke refutes the theory of pre-existence by saying that if a man has no memory at all of his previous existence, if he has "a consciousness that *cannot* reach beyond this new state," then he is not the same person who led the previous existence since "personal identity [reaches] no further than consciousness reaches." [13] Wordsworth's answer is to blur the line between remembering and forgetting, to introduce a notion of unconscious memory. By combining memory and association, Wordsworth sets the Lockean system in motion, infusing it with vitality, surrounding it with mystery, and carrying the mind back beyond conscious memory to the "dawn of being" where it is undistinguishable from its first sensation.

Memory becomes in Wordsworth the instrument of the associative or transforming power. It is because we see with stereoscopic vision—as Roger Shattuck puts it in speaking, in *Proust's Binoculars*, of Proust's use of memory—it is because partly we see the tree before us and partly we see all the trees we have ever seen that we see from outside and inside and have not sensations but experiences.[14] With the "impressions" before him, says Wordsworth in *The Excursion*,

> would he still compare
> All his remembrances, thoughts, shapes and forms;
> And, being still unsatisfied with aught
> Of dimmer character, he thence attained
> An active power to fasten images
> Upon his brain; and on their pictured lines
> Intensely brooded, even till they acquired
> The liveliness of dreams.   (1.141–148)

That is the meaning of the crucial line in "Tintern Abbey": "The picture of the mind revives again." Wordsworth sees the present landscape through his mental picture of the landscape five years earlier. Because he discovers continuity in the disparate pictures through a principle of growth, he becomes aware of the pattern of his life—he binds his apparently disparate days together. He may be said to evolve his soul in becoming aware that his soul evolves. Included in the present experience is Wordsworth's sense that he will in future feed upon it, just as in the intervening five years he has fed on his last visit to this place. The experience includes, in other words, the consciousness of laying up treasure —not in heaven but in the memory. It is the point of "Tintern Abbey," "Immortality Ode," and *The Prelude* that this spiritual storehouse of memory *is* our soul.

In one of the earliest written passages of *The Prelude*, one of those passages that must have helped Wordsworth find his theme, the poet thanks nature, in a tone of religious solemnity, for having from his "first dawn / Of childhood" intertwined for him "The passions that build up our human soul" (1.405–407).[15] The whole poem traces this building-up process, but the words *soul* and *imagination* are used interchangeably and Wordsworth speaks more often of the building-up of imagination. That is because the poet or man of imagination is being used to epitomize a psychological process.

The poet, we are being told, is more spiritual than the rest of us because he *remembers* more than we do—though his remembering is often spoken of as a kind of forgetting: "By such forgetfulness the soul becomes, / Words cannot say how beautiful" (*Recluse* 1.297–298). The poet filters a present experience back through memory and the unconscious river in his veins—Wordsworth habitually speaks of thought as flowing in and out of the veins—to the external river that was his first sensation. That is why the poet can respond to the world and see it symbolically. That is why seeing is better than faith—it is revelation. "Nor did he believe,— he *saw*," says Wordsworth of the poetical Pedlar in *The Excursion* (1.232).

Wordsworth achieves his symbolic effects through a regression in the mind of the observer and in the object observed. He makes the human figure seem to evolve out of and pass back into the landscape—as in "The Thorn" and the Lucy poems, including "Lucy Gray." And he makes the landscape itself, in his most striking effects, seem to evolve out of water. In "Resolution and Independence," the old leech gatherer is seen by a pool. He is so old that he seems to hang on to life by a thread; and the observer understands this by carrying the old man's existence back to the line between the inanimate and the animate. The observer sees the old man as like a huge stone that seems almost alive because you cannot imagine how it got where it is, or as like a sea beast that at first seems part of the rock on which it lies. He is—if you assimi-

late this poem, as Geoffrey Hartman has so beautifully done, to
the recurrent imagery of *The Prelude*—like something left behind
by the inland sea that once covered the landscape.[16] Because the
old man is seen through the eye of unconscious racial memory, he
is transformed into an archetype of human endurance capable of
alleviating the observer's distress.

In one of the epiphanies or "spots of time" of *The Prelude*,
Book XII, Wordsworth recalls how as a boy he fled in terror from a
low place, where a murderer had been hanged, to a hill where he
saw a pool and a girl approaching it, bearing a pitcher on her head,
her garments blowing in the wind. Through the conjunction with
water and wind, the girl turns for the boy into an archetypal figure
who transforms the unpleasant experience into a pleasant one; so
that in later years, when Wordsworth was courting Mary Hutchin-
son, he often returned with her to this place, finding in "the
naked pool and dreary crags" a "spirit of pleasure and youth's
golden gleam" (264, 266). Here and elsewhere in Wordsworth—
the same female figure with a basket on her head is remembered
through water imagery in "The Two April Mornings"—water and
memory, water as perhaps the counterpart of memory, turn the individual event into an archetype. And it is through archetypalization that turbulence and pain are turned into spiritual treasure,
into the recognition of that surrounding aura of pleasurable tranquillity which is soul. "How strange," says Wordsworth in speaking of soul-making,

> that all
> The terrors, pains, and early miseries,
> Regrets, vexations, lassitudes interfused
> Within my mind, should e'er have borne a part,
> And that a needful part in making up
> The calm existence that is mine when I
> Am worthy of myself!   (1.344–350)

The transformation of pain into pleasure is achieved through
archetypalization and objectification. The terrifying boyhood ex-

perience of Book xii passes into the landscape, making it a pleasant and spiritually rewarding place to return to. Wordsworth says that "The sands of Westmoreland, the creeks and bays / Of Cumbria's rocky limits" can tell of his boyhood epiphanies; and that, conversely,

> The scenes which were a witness of that joy
> Remained in their substantial lineaments
> Depicted on the brain,
>
> (1.567–568, 599–601)

that he remembered those early experiences as places.

The pleasurable tranquillity that is soul exists outside us as well as inside; it exists in those places hallowed by significant experiences. Place, in Wordsworth, is the spatial projection of psyche, because it is the repository of memory.[17] We can understand the relation in Wordsworth between mind and nature, once we understand that Wordsworth evolves his soul or sense of identity as he identifies more and more such hallowed places. We can understand the relation in Wordsworth between the themes of memory and growing up, once we understand that for Wordsworth you advance in life by travelling back again to the beginning, by reassessing your life, by binding your days together anew.

In Coleridge's periodical *The Friend*, Wordsworth answers a conservative attack on the belief in progress, by saying that in the progress of the species and the individual mind we must often move backward in order to move forward. Progress

> neither is nor can be like that of a Roman road in a right line. It may be more justly compared to that of a river, which, both in its smaller reaches and larger turnings, is frequently forced back towards its fountains by objects which can not otherwise be eluded or overcome; yet with an accompanying impulse that will insure its advancement hereafter, it is either gaining strength every hour, or conquering in secret some difficulty, by a labor that contributes as effectually to further it in its course, as when it moves forward uninterrupted in a line.

And Coleridge in *The Friend* uses "My Heart Leaps Up," the poem in which Wordsworth speaks of binding his days together, to support his idea that we must in growing up be able to correct the delusions of our childhood without repudiating the child who held them.

> If men laugh at the falsehoods that were imposed on themselves during their childhood, it is because they are not good and wise enough to contemplate the past in the present, and so to produce by a virtuous and thoughtful sensibility that continuity in their self-consciousness, which nature has made the law of their animal life. Ingratitude, sensuality, and hardness of heart, all flow from this source. Men are ungrateful to others only when they have ceased to look back on their former selves with joy and tenderness. They exist in fragments. Annihilated as to the past, they are dead to the future, or seek for the proofs of it everywhere, not only (where alone they can be found) in themselves.[18]

The old Pedlar of *The Excursion* shows that he has bound his days together; for age has

> not tamed his eye; that, under brows
> Shaggy and grey, had meanings which it brought
> From years of youth; which, like a Being made
> Of many Beings, he had wondrous skill
> To blend with knowledge of the years to come,
> Human, or such as lie beyond the grave.
>
> (1.428–433)

Because "like a Being made / Of many Beings," he possesses his past, he possesses the future too and seems to transcend time. The same is true of old Matthew in "The Two April Mornings," who, in the moment when he was able to immerse himself completely in the stream of time by remembering and reconciling himself to his daughter's death, became for the young narrator immortal:

> Matthew is in his grave, yet now,
> Methinks, I see him stand,

As at that moment, with a bough
Of wilding in his hand.

In *The Prelude*'s climactic "spot of time," the epiphany on Mt.
Snowdon in Book xiv, the whole world seems under moonlight to
be returned to water. The mist below is a silent sea, the hills
around static billows; and this illusory sea stretches out into the
real Atlantic. The optical illusion is substantiated when, through a
rift in the mist, Wordsworth hears the roar of inland waters. The
movement from sight to sound is always in Wordsworth a movement backward to the beginning of things, to sensation and the
sentiment of Being; later in Book xiv, Wordsworth says that he
has in *The Prelude* traced the stream of imagination back from
"light / And open day" to "the blind cavern whence is faintly
heard / Its natal murmur" (195–197). Wordsworth understands,
therefore, that he has had on Mt. Snowdon an epiphany of pure
imagination or pure potentiality. He has beheld, in the moon
over the waters, "the emblem of a mind" brooding over the abyss
—waiting, like Cod in the opening passage of *Paradise Lost*, to
bring forth the world. Wordsworth transcends even the beginning
of things by moving back from sight to sound and then to an inextricable blending of sight and sound:

> the emblem of a mind
> That feeds upon infinity, that broods
> Over the dark abyss, intent to hear
> Its voices issuing forth to silent light
> In one continuous stream.   (70–74)

"This," says Wordsworth, "is the very spirit" with which
"higher" or imaginative "minds" deal "With the whole compass
of the universe" (90–93). Confronted with sensory experience,
the poetical man travels back *that far* in order to perceive it imagi-
natively. He re-creates the world in his imagination; [19] so that he
can return to the scene before him, imposing upon it the picture
in his mind and thus finding there the surrounding aura of calm

that is his soul. Only by travelling back to the beginning can we achieve the "repose / In moral judgments," which is a sign that we have bound our ideas up with our primitive sensations. In borrowing, to describe the repose or calm, words of Holy Scripture, in describing it as "that peace / Which passeth understanding" (126–128), Wordsworth shows that he considers his naturalistic revelation to be not only the equivalent of the Platonic idea, but this time the equivalent of Christian revelation itself.

THE
VICTORIAN
IDEA
OF CULTURE

To understand what the Victorian age means to us today, let us take the case of E. M. Forster. Two recent books, discussed in my essay on Forster, see the story of his family as characteristic of the century-long migration of English liberal intellectuals from Clapham to Bloomsbury. Forster is the great-grandson of the Evangelical and Utilitarian M.P., Henry Thornton of Clapham; and Clapham, near London, was at the beginning of the nineteenth century the home of the so-called Clapham Sect wealthy lay leaders of the Evangelical or Low Church reforming party within the Church of England. At Clapham resided Hannah More, who wrote pious tracts and did philanthropic work among the poor, and William Wilberforce, who led the campaign to abolish the slave trade and was aided in the campaign by such other residents as Zachary Macaulay, father of Thomas Babington, later Lord Macaulay, and James Stephen, grandfather of Leslie Stephen and great-grandfather of Virginia Woolf. These families gradually connected through marriages with Trevelyans, Huxleys, Arnolds, Darwins, Keyneses, Stracheys—all the families which, according to

Noel Annan in his biography of Leslie Stephen, constitute the intellectual aristocracy of modern England.

The point is that in the early nineteenth century the upper middle-class elite believed in piety, reform of Church and State, moral action and laissez-faire economics. Their early twentieth-century descendants, however, as represented by the so-called Bloomsbury Group (Leslie Stephen's four children formed the nucleus; Lytton Strachey and J. M. Keynes belonged; Forster was a frequent visitor), disbelieved in religion and moral action, and did believe in government regulation or ownership of industry and in refinement of sensibility. Between Clapham and Bloomsbury stands Matthew Arnold with his admonition to liberals to be less Hebraic or moral and more Hellenic or aesthetic; for the Victorian experience had shown that moral action without self-understanding and inner refinement resulted in the hypocrisy and the damaging forms of philanthropy Dickens is so good at exposing. Thus Bloomsbury's favorite philosopher, G. E. Moore, taught that nothing mattered but "states of mind." Forster himself, in *Two Cheers for Democracy*, sums up the paradoxical position of liberal intellectuals nowadays in Britain and America. We believe in government regulation of the economy, he suggests, but in a laissez-faire of the spirit; we believe in political democracy, but in an aristocracy of the spirit.[1] Since this is the position toward which the whole Victorian literary enterprise has led us, we can see why Victorian literature matters. And, indeed, the concerted revaluation of the period that has gone on since 1940 has quite reversed the old sneering attitude exemplified by Lytton Strachey's *Eminent Victorians* (1918).

The order of perception that lay behind Arnold's attack is expressed by the remark of Arnold's contemporary, Walter Bagehot, that "Nothing is more unpleasant than a virtuous person with a mean mind. A highly developed moral nature joined to an undeveloped intellectual nature, an undeveloped artistic nature, is of necessity repulsive."[2] In the 1850's, the younger members of the prosperous middle class were becoming aware of the narrowness and meagreness of the middle-class tradition. The word "Victorian" or "Early Victorian" began at this time to appear in its pejorative sense, to refer to the middle-class Evangelical and Utilitarian spirit. Since the best Victorian writers were on the whole anti-"Victorian," we have to read backwards from their writings to discern the assumptions and tastes of the articulate public.

Thomas Babington Macaulay is the one outstanding writer who does speak for the middle class, just because he steered a Whiggish course between the Evangelical Toryism of his father, on the one side, and, on the other, the democratic politics and religious agnosticism of the Benthamites. Macaulay believed like the Benthamites in progress and laissez-faire, but was more genial, literary, conventional and far less philosophical than they. He was in these respects—in others, he was Augustan and aristocratic through his connection with the Whig nobility—closer to popular thinking than the Benthamites. In his passion for political liberty, Macaulay represents the best of the middle-class spirit. But in his identification of reason with common sense and in his smug satisfaction with the age because it showed numerical increase in population and wealth, he displays the attitudes Arnold was to stigmatize as Philistine ("a Philistine of genius," A. L. Rowse calls Macaulay). To understand the side against which the literary men were reacting, read Macaulay's attack in 1830 on Southey's book, *Sir Thomas More; or Colloquies on the Progress and Prospects of Society.*

Southey and the other two Lake poets, Wordsworth and Coleridge, were considered renegades, because they had started in the 1790's as radicals, supporters of the French Revolution, and later turned into Tories. But leaving aside their personal crotchets, they are, I think, to be understood as the first Victorians, in that they realized long before Queen Victoria's accession that the nature of the enemy had changed—that the enemy was no longer feudalism but rather the laissez-faire industrialism that threatened to destroy the countryside and men's souls. From what Macaulay says about

Southey and what Mill in "Coleridge" (1840) says about Coleridge, we see the makings of a peculiarly Victorian phenomenon—that the movement against laissez-faire and toward the present-day welfare state came largely from the right, from conservatives harking back nostalgically to a unified and more humane agrarian order. In the early Carlyle of *Sartor Resartus* (1833–1834) and *Past and Present* (1843), we see a radical conservatism; for Carlyle wanted radical institutional changes in order to revivify the permanent responsibility of all societies to look after the physical, moral and spiritual welfare of their citizens. The economists were mistaken, said Carlyle, in supposing that they had found a new formula through which society could now shirk its responsibility, could send its citizens into the "free market" with the pious hope that the general good would somehow be served if each man looked after his own interest without minding the other fellow's.

The characteristics we think of as Victorian were well established by the time of the Queen's accession in 1837. Some historians consider the era as starting with the 1832 Reform Bill, which opened the way for the eventual political ascendancy of the middle class and ushered in a rapid succession of legislative reforms. Certainly the laissez-faire ideology was fully developed by 1832; whereas serious regulation of industry began with the Factory Act of 1833—which was the first act regulating hours and conditions of work that had teeth in it, because it provided for inspection. There followed, in counterpoint to a continued lifting of controls, a succession of regulatory laws; it was the pro-laissez-faire Benthamites, paradoxically, who had prepared the administrative apparatus that made regulation possible. Victoria's reign saw, therefore, in what was finally to prove to be the main current, a steady retreat from laissez-faire. Again, if we associate Victorianism with prudery, gloomy Sundays, and fear of the senses, pleasure and art—with, in other words, the Evangelical spirit—then it is also true that the Evangelical spirit had triumphed by 1833, the year of Wilberforce's death and the Abolition of Slavery, and that Victoria's reign saw a slow retreat from it, a retreat that became apparent when aestheticism developed after the mid-century into a conspicuous cultural force. By the 1890's the cultivated minority was in full rebellion against prudery.

The apparent exception to the above line of development is the Free Trade principle, which did not win out until 1846 with the repeal of the Corn Laws, the tariff on wheat that seemed to protect the aristocratic or landed interest. The Free Trade principle, which had acquired the magical sanction of a religious dogma, maintained its ascendancy for the rest of the century even though British agriculture suffered badly in the last three decades from the competition of American wheat.

Another Victorian characteristic, well established before the Queen's accession, resulted from the unprecedented statistical surveys that accompanied the reform movement of the thirties. The thirties was the decade of the Blue Books, the reports of Parliamentary Committees or Royal Commissions on every aspect of English life except agriculture. Engels and Marx, who settled in England in 1849 (Engels had already visited in 1843-1844), used these Blue Books—Engels for *The Condition of the Working Class in England in 1844* and Marx for *Das Kapital*, the first volume of which was published in 1867. The guiding spirit behind the Blue Books was that of Bentham and his Philosophic Radicals or Utilitarians; and they, through the Blue Books, taught the English reading public to worship—as Dickens was to put it satirically in *Hard Times*—"Facts . . . Facts . . . Facts."

The Philistine worship of facts went along with a literary reaction against Byronism that followed Byron's death in 1824. The literary reaction, as summed up by Carlyle's injunction in *Sartor*, "Close thy Byron; open thy Goethe," was against self-preoccupation and for the social responsibility that Wilhelm Meister and Faust finally arrive at. As summed up by Sir Henry Taylor in the Preface to his verse drama *Philip Van Artevelde* (1834), the reaction was against too much feeling and imagination at the expense of realism, intellect and morality. Passing on to Shelley, Taylor condemns him for a too exclusive pursuit of beauty and for a visionary quality that presents us forms "never to be seen through the mere medium of eyesight."

It was into this hostile atmosphere that Tennyson and Browning sent their still romantic poems of 1830, with unhappy results. Tennyson, particularly, wavered throughout his career between his impulse to write poetry of private sensation and his genuine interest in writing on public issues and joining in the march of progress. In reviewing Tennyson's 1830 *Poems*, Arthur Hallam praises Tennyson for just the qualities Taylor condemns in Shelley; for Hallam classes Tennyson with Keats and Shelley, with "poets of sensation" as distinguished from a "reflective" poet like Wordsworth. Hallam's position was taken up again in the aesthetic movement—especially the later phase, beginning with Pater in the seventies, that defined itself in opposition to ideas and dogmatic commitments. Yeats, in his essay "Art and Ideas" (1913), draws a line from Shelley and Keats through early Tennyson and the Pre-Raphaelites (who preferred early Tennyson) to the poets of the nineties and the twentieth-century poetry of Yeats himself. The opposing impulses that Tennyson along with Browning and Arnold contained within themselves were polarized by the end of the century between, on the one hand, the extreme aestheticism of Yeats and his friends, the poets of the nineties, who sought to empty their poetry of content, and, on the other hand, the socially responsible naturalism of Ibsen and Shaw. Yeats in his *Autobiography* (1938) writes that he and his friends could not escape the antithetical Ibsen, because "we had the same enemies." The enemies were, of course, the middle-class Philistines—which suggests that both sides were revolutionary and had in common a principle of progress opposed to that of the Philistines, a principle based on more complex criteria than the rise in national wealth and population. To this larger principle of progress, the nineteenth century gave the elusive name of "culture."

In the Introduction to his important book, *Culture and Society 1780–1950*, Raymond Williams lists five key words that either came into common use or acquired new meanings at the turn of the nineteenth century. From these words, changes in life and thought can be charted. And of these words—*industry, democracy, class* (rather than *rank*), *art* (as a specialized activity superior to all other human skills), and *culture*—the last presents the most important and complex cluster of concepts. Williams goes on in the rest of the book to investigate the development and ramifications of the idea of culture through studies of major figures from Burke through the Victorians to Lawrence, Eliot, the Marxist critics and Orwell. He locates the idea of culture in the principle held in common by such contrasting pairs as the late eighteenth-century conservative Burke and the radical Cobbett; or the early nineteenth-century Tory Southey and socialist Robert Owen. Both sides "attacked the new [industrializing] England from their experience of the old England," and were concerned with what had been lost.

Such reconciliation of opposites relates to John Stuart Mill's advice to his contemporaries, in the essay on Coleridge, to "master the premises and combine the methods" of Bentham and Coleridge. Bentham was a radical, utterly irreverent of the past, who thought all laws and institutions ought to be subjected to the test of utility, "the greatest happiness of the greatest number"; while the later Coleridge, the Coleridge of the prose writings who exercised so much influence on the Victorians, was a romantic conservative, who was mainly out to rehabilitate old institutions. By absorbing into his own inherited Benthamism the opposite Coleridgian view, Mill worked out for himself what was to be the characteristic Victorian synthesis—the absorption, that is, into a progressivist philosophy of a new respect for the past and for those institutions and values of the past that could not have been what the Benthamites thought them, mere frauds, since they had engaged the best minds and hearts of so many centuries.

When Mill goes on to say that the Germano-Coleridgian school has made the largest contribution "towards the philosophy of human culture," he means that the school of Herder and Goethe, with its influence on Michelet in France and Coleridge in England, has taught us to view alien societies, whether past or present, as manifestations of national *character* at a particular phase of development. Societies are not, in other words, to be judged by a fixed abstract standard, but are to be understood as *characteristic* and therefore self-justifying—once we understand how they came to be as they are and how their parts cohere to make an organism adapted to its geographical and historical environment.[3]

I use the biological metaphor to make a point Mill does not make—that the central idea of the nineteenth century is the organicist or evolutionary idea, launched in England by Burke's answer to the French Revolutionists who wanted to wipe out the past and start over with an abstract blueprint for the perfect society. Burke's answer was to say that the state is in some respects like a plant, that it is organized according to a living principle of continuity that cannot be abrogated and that transforms separate persons into a People—into an entity greater than and different from the sum of its parts. The state is an artificial creation, but one which functions for man, who is a reasonable being, *like* a natural organism—for "Art is man's nature." [4]

That paradox of Burke's—"Art is man's nature"—helps us understand the nineteenth-century concept of culture—the concept behind the attempt of the Victorians to reconcile change with continuity and order. The Latin *cultura* means cultivation of the soil; and the obvious emphasis, the emphasis one still finds in Arnold, is on education, on the things man adds to nature. But Arnold is aware that culture is also an unconscious inevitable growth; and Carlyle insists that the principles that really hold society together are unconscious.

In our own time, when sociologists, anthropologists and depth psychologists have further expanded the concept of culture, the word is seldom used in serious discussions to mean *belles lettres*, but comprehends every characterizing aspect of a people, their *whole* way of life. The most trivial characteristics—the ones of which we are not conscious—may be most fundamental, because indicative of that internal life of a people that survives political change. It is internality, if not subconsciousness, that stands behind Coleridge's distinction between cultivation or culture and civilization: "a nation can never be a too cultivated, but may easily become an over-civilized, race"; or behind Mill's criticism of Bentham: "Man is never recognized by Bentham as a being capable of pursuing spiritual perfection as an end." [5] T. S. Eliot, however, has both internality and subconsciousness in mind in *Notes towards the Definition of Culture*. Since "culture cannot altogether be brought to consciousness," says Eliot, it cannot be dominated or directed by politics or education. "The culture of which we are wholly conscious is never the whole of culture: the effective culture is that which is directing the activities of those who are manipulating that which they *call* culture." [6] Like Burke, Eliot uses the concept of culture to oppose the engineered or totally manipulated society.

One has to understand that the word *culture* was from the beginning charged with a world-view and a battle cry. In a revolutionary age, the word was used to define a principle of continuity underlying political, economic and even social change. It was used in an industrial age, which measured progress by numbers, to ask about the *quality* of life—especially since quality seemed to be declining. Since the economy required specialization and dehumanization, the word *culture* was invoked as an argument for the harmonious development of all our human faculties. Since the dominating middle class viewed art as useless and therefore as a mere luxury product, the antithetical concept of culture came to include the idea that the art of a period is an index to its quality and that aesthetic judgments are therefore inextricably related to moral and social judgments. This was the lesson taught, as regards architecture and the visual arts, by Pugin, Ruskin and Morris; and, as regards literature, by Matthew Arnold. "For the creation of a master-work of literature," says Arnold, "two powers must concur, the power of the man and the power of the moment, and the man is not enough without the moment; the creative power has, for its happy exercise, appointed elements, and those elements are not in its own control." Style came to be regarded as organic to a society and therefore as an index to its real or subconscious character.

Because the Victorians' attack on their own age is so largely expressed through the concept of culture, the literature of the age is inextricably connected with its histories and social criticism. For the concept of culture was the product of the literary mind when it was turned upon the unprecedented conditions of the nineteenth century. Indeed the literary mind, with its memory of other world-views and of "the best [in Arnold's words] that is known and thought in the world," offered the one hope of escape, that was not a mere return to stale orthodoxy, from the latest shibboleths—"the greatest happiness of the greatest number" or "doing as you like with your own."

It took a mind stored with cultural memory to see, as Coleridge does, how unprecedentedly brutal was the economists' justification of depressions as self-regulating machinery to help "things find their level."

> But persons are not things—but man does not find his level. Neither in body nor in soul does the man find his level. . . . Be it that plenty has returned and that trade has once more become brisk and stirring: go, ask the overseer, and question the parish doctor, whether the workman's health and temperance with the staid and respectful manners best taught by the inward dignity of conscious self-support, have found their level again! [7]

It took a mind stored with cultural memory to see, as Carlyle does in the powerful opening chapter of *Past and Present*, that England in the "hungry forties" lay under a Midas enchantment—dying of starvation with wealth all around. The enchantment was the paralyzing laissez-faire dogma that forbade tampering with the free market; so that men could not reach out and distribute the wealth they were producing. It required cultural memory to see in the case of the pauper Wragg who strangled her unwanted baby on the bleak Mapperley Hills, to see in the case, as Arnold does in the essay I have been quoting, not so much the age-old story of poverty but, through the ugliness of the names and setting and the impersonal newspaper account, an unprecedentedly dismal cultural situation.

In this essay, "The Function of Criticism at the Present Time," Arnold means by "criticism" just such a turning of the literary mind upon public affairs. Not only has the literary mind access to a high and wide tradition by which to judge the current scene, but it has the "disinterestedness," the ability to play freely with ideas and possibilities, which is the peculiar reward of literary study. Because of this disinterestedness, the literary mind can give assent to opposite positions—as, according to Arnold, Burke did when he concluded his arguments against the French Revolution as follows:

> "If a great change is to be made in human affairs, the minds of men will be fitted to it; the general opinions and feelings will draw that way. Every fear, every hope will forward it; and then they who persist in opposing this mighty current in human affairs, will appear rather to resist the decrees of Providence itself, than the mere designs of men. They will not be resolute and firm, but perverse and obstinate." [8]

Like Arnold, who though a liberal spent most of his career criticizing liberals, Burke paid allegiance to a principle of culture that can be served by a properly informed liberal or conservative position. The conservative Coleridge, for example, influenced the Christian Socialist and the Broad Church or liberal Anglican movements. And Arnold, in *Culture and Anarchy* (1869), connects the working-class movement of the sixties with Newman's

Oxford or High Church movement which, in promoting thirty years earlier the dogmatic, Catholic character of Anglicanism, helped undermine the Protestant, liberal individualism of the middle class.[9]

Perhaps the most important advantage of the literary mind is that its figurative way of reading events and using language enables it to deal at once with external and internal matters. This advantage accounts for a peculiar phenomenon of the age. I mean the so-called Victorian prophets or sages—prose writers like Carlyle, Newman, Arnold, Ruskin (I would add Pater and the discursive Morris; Shaw and Lawrence are in the same tradition) who, whether they wrote on history, or on political, social or economic subjects, religion, literature or the visual arts, wrote under a governing principle of culture that connected any one of these subjects with all the others and with a demand for action, either personal or social. The most distinctive things about these discursive prose writings is that they ranked with the poetry and fiction of the age as literature.

In a brilliant introduction to his book, *The Victorian Sage*, John Holloway shows why these discursive writings can be regarded as literature. Like the poet and novelist, the Victorian sage persuades not by logical argument but by projecting a coherent vision of life into which his argument fits. "The methods traced here persuade because they clarify, and clarify because they are organic to a view presented not by one thread of logical argument alone, but by the whole weave of a book." To judge the argument, "one must have a critic's sense of how the parts of a book unite in what is not a logical unity." The views of the Victorian sages cannot be judged by summaries; for "what gave their views life and meaning lay in the actual words of the original . . . to work by quickening the reader to a new capacity for experience is to work in the mode of the artist in words." Thus Holloway extends the term *Victorian sage* to cover novelists like Disraeli, George Eliot and Hardy, who deal with the same subjects as the discursive writers through "illustrative incidents in a story" analogous to the latter's "illustrative examples in an argument." [10] Indeed, all the major poets and novelists dealt like the Victorian sages with the same cluster of subjects, subjects related to each other through a governing concept of culture.

Victorian writers dealt with the fragmentation of life in the nineteenth century, just because they carried in their heads an ideal of cultural unity. But the ideal in their heads was itself a result of fragmentation, of their being forced to internalize those values of the superseded agrarian, aristocratic and Christian society, the loss of which in the public domain produced the feeling of fragmentation. Thus the Victorian writers established what remains the special knack of modern intellectuals—the knack of inhabiting two or more cultures at the same time. We can appreciate in literary or historical discussion the virtues of noblemen and peasants, or of an age of faith, or of exotically primitive peoples, at the same time that we vote for more democracy and social welfare and, crowning irony, the industrialization of agrarian societies. That is how we arrive at the paradoxical position described by E. M. Forster. For we have appropriated to the realm of the spirit the aristocratic pursuit of distinction and the bold individualism of the laissez-faire principle, even though we have abolished the aristocracy from our political life and the laissez-faire principle from our economic life.

The Victorian writers have taught us that culture can and should be antithetical to the prevailing ideology—not so much to destroy the ideology (though that may at times be necessary) as to complete it. In teaching us that the mind must inhabit and judge from a much larger sphere than any ideology can supply, the Victorian writers have bequeathed us the crucial principle by which societies in our time might be differentiated. For now that in politics the democratic *principle* is universally acknowledged even if it is not universally in effect, and now that the distinction is dissolving between capitalist and socialist economies, the crucial difference ought to be between open and closed societies—between societies that respect the autonomy of culture and those that use culture to close up all avenues of intellectual escape, to reinforce the dreary clichés of political and economic bosses.

I say *ought to,* because the concept of culture is hard to maintain after all we have been through in the first half of the twentieth century. Auschwitz might be read as a portent of the future; and if we read it so, what happens to our faith in the organically inevitable enlargement of consciousness? Besides, the organic metaphor, which derives everything from the soil, may be inappropriate to a time when man is taking off from Earth itself. More immediately discouraging is the spectacle of the open societies of the West, where the autonomy of culture has led to a binge of "consumerism" and a taste for intellectual pap—to a freely chosen intellectual sleep.

Orwell's *Nineteen Eighty-Four* projects the nightmare future of a technologically advanced socialist society without culture—without the individuality, spirituality and intellectual freedom, without the whole heritage of the past that originally produced the technology and socialism. To achieve total tyranny, to make consciousness identical with ideology, the party reduces the area of private life by discouraging sexual and family love, and reduces the range of consciousness by reducing available vocabulary and obliterating all memory of the past. The one glimmer of hope is in the hero, an obsolete man who still has some primitive instincts and some cultural memory. Similarly, to the extent that we can think optimistically about the future, our thoughts are necessarily based on the cluster of ideas connected with the word *culture*—ideas that give coherence to the main body of nineteenth- and twentieth-century literature.

THE
DYNAMIC UNITY
OF
IN MEMORIAM

In *Science and the Modern World,* Alfred North Whitehead compares Tennyson's *In Memoriam* to Milton's *Paradise
Lost* and Pope's *Essay on Man,* in that *In Memoriam* "exactly,"
like these earlier long poems, "expressed the character of its period." Its period runs from 1833—when Tennyson's gifted young
friend Arthur Hallam died suddenly in Vienna, and Tennyson to
express his grief began writing the individual lyrics—to 1850, when
the lyrics written during the intervening seventeen years were finally organized and published as presumably one long poem. The mid-
Victorian poem is especially comparable to the early eighteenth-
century *Essay on Man,* because Tennyson like Pope summarizes the
scientific knowledge of his time and relates it to questions of religious and moral judgment. Pope, however, is optimistic about the
implications of Newtonian physics; whereas Tennyson, who was
thinking about geology, biology and the new astronomy, is for
most of the poem pessimistic. The difference is that for the Victorians, scientific knowledge was antithetical to, rather than pro-
ductive of, a religious and ethical position. And it is this antithesis

—this characteristically Victorian controversy between science and religious faith—that Whitehead had in mind in speaking of *In Memoriam* as expressive of its age.

In composing an elegy for Arthur Hallam who died before he could fulfill his promise of a brilliant political career, Tennyson faced the question of all elegists. If this can happen, what is the value of life? Just as in Milton's elegy, *Lycidas*, this question leads to general questions of the age (in Milton, the bad state of the church); so, to an even greater degree, in Tennyson. The difference is that Milton could draw upon his age—upon its Renaissance humanistic and its Christian tradition—for an answer. But Tennyson could not easily take over a Christian or even a humanistic answer, because the latest science—mainly Lyell's geology, which taught the vastness of geological time and the extinction of species, and the Herschels' astronomy, which demoted the sun to a minor star in our galaxy and taught the evolution of stars out of nebulae—made it difficult to believe in a purposeful, moral universe, or in the importance of man, much less individual man. If man, too, the poet asks, were to be "seal'd within the iron hills," were to leave as his only trace fossils in the rocks, what hope for the immortality of Hallam's soul or for the enduring value of one's love for him? One could no longer, like the Deists and Wordsworthians, find evidence in nature for the existence of God. But one could—these are the answers Tennyson arrives at—rely on the testimony of the heart and see, in the natural evolution of species, an analogue to social progress and man's spiritual evolution. Thus, Tennyson anticipated the discussion that was to follow the publication of Darwin's *Origin of Species* in 1859.

But the age in which he found himself was inimical to an answer. The age had to be overcome. Tennyson does, it is true, finally draw upon answers already prepared by Carlyle and by Coleridge—Coleridge as filtered through that society founded by Coleridgians, the Cambridge Apostles, to which both he and Hallam had belonged. But Tennyson makes these earlier answers his own, because he took science more seriously, knew much more about it, and coped with a more modern science than did Coleridge and Carlyle. Tennyson wins his victory—if we agree that he wins it— over far more intractable material than theirs. In Memoriam is generally called—and I have so called it—a mid-Victorian poem. But it derived from the early Victorian period, the tormented 1830's and 40's. In the questions it raised and the answers it proposed, In Memoriam helped shape the affirmative attitudes that characterized the relatively complacent mid-Victorian period—the period that began about the time In Memoriam appeared in 1850.

That is why In Memoriam came under attack as later generations reacted against the mid-Victorian affirmations—against what G. K. Chesterton, writing in 1913, called "the Victorian compromise," [1] in this case the compromise between science and religion. Victorian humanists, a liberal Anglican like F. D. Maurice, a skeptic like Henry Sidgwick, together with leading scientists, Sir John Herschel and others, thought Tennyson had managed to re-establish the possibilities of faith precisely by taking into account the scientific difficulties and "through almost the agonies of a death struggle." [2] But in 1923, Hugh I'Anson Faussett attacked Tennyson's simpleminded and timid attempt to reconcile science and religion as doing justice to neither. "The synthesis which Tennyson affected was too easy and superficial to excite in him either profound emotion or passionate thought, the two forces out of which poetry is born. He never faced the darkness, and fought his way out into daylight, but . . . [remained] safe in the citadel of traditional belief." [3] Harold Nicolson, who published in that year the book that started the modern rehabilitation of Tennyson, considers that Tennyson did face the darkness. Nicolson finds the emotion profound, inasmuch as the emotion is despair, but objects to the structure, "the artificially constructed synthesis," that betokens a movement toward affirmation. [4]

T. S. Eliot carries the appreciation of Tennyson up through In Memoriam, when in his essay of 1936 he calls it the work in

which "Tennyson finds full expression." But Eliot, too, is interested in *In Memoriam* as a poem of despair. "I get a very different
impression from *In Memoriam* from that which Tennyson's contemporaries seem to have got. It is of a very much more interesting and tragic Tennyson." Tennyson's feelings were more honest
than his thought, and therefore *In Memoriam* is a religious poem,
not "because of the quality of its faith, but because of the quality
of its doubt. Its faith is a poor thing, but its doubt is a very intense
experience. *In Memoriam* is a poem of despair, but of despair of a
religious kind." And Eliot says about *In Memoriam* a kind of
thing that he has said about his own poem of religious despair,
The Waste Land. "It happens now and then that a poet by some
strange accident expresses the mood of his generation, at the same
time that he is expressing a mood of his own which is quite remote from that of his generation." [5] Now *The Waste Land* is a
poem that stands up against the first two decades of the twentieth
century, that exposes the boredom and terror of the age's faithless-
ness. And to the extent that *In Memoriam* is about the 1830's and
40's, it stands up against the age—makes the age face the religious
impasse to which it has been brought by all the revolutionary forces
of the age but mainly by science.

When on the first Christmas after Hallam's death the Tennysons sing the traditional hymns, teaching that the dead "do not
die / Nor lose their mortal sympathy" (xxx), it is clear that they
cannot really believe these words. And in the moving section that
follows, "When Lazarus left his charnel-cave, / And home to
Mary's house return'd," we are told that even Lazarus who returned from the grave has left no record of what it was like there.
His sister Mary, whose "eyes," we are told in the next section, "are
homes of silent prayer," is content to accept without question the
miracle of resurrection and adore the Savior who wrought it. And
in the section following, the sophisticated reader is told not to de-
spise those present-day Marys whose faith is simple and literal; but
it is clear that the present-day Marys are not modern, have not got
the age in their bones.

Not only has Christianity been exploded; so has its romantic substitute—the faith in the benevolent life of nature. It is because the romantic faith is the most proximate and potent that the scientific devaluation of nature plays so important a part in this poem. Section III, in which Sorrow whispers conclusions drawn from the new astronomy, marks the crucial dividing line between romantic and modern nature poetry.

> "The stars," she whispers, "blindly run;
> A web is wov'n across the sky;
> From out waste places comes a cry,
> And murmurs from the dying sun:
>
> "And all the phantom, Nature, stands—
> With all the music in her tone,
> A hollow echo of my own,—
> A hollow form with empty hands." [6]

The nature that used to echo Wordsworthian joy has lost all vitality; it is now a ghost, echoing Sorrow's voice and teaching only death. "A web is wov'n across the sky" suggests that nature now conceals, instead of revealing, God.

This theme is taken up again in section LVI, the most famous of the nature poems. Having in the previous section come full circle from the Wordsworthian belief in God in nature:

> Are God and Nature then at strife,
> That Nature lends such evil dreams?
> So careful of the type she seems,
> So careless of the single life;

Tennyson now remembers Lyell's fossils in the rocks:

> "So careful of the type?" but no.
> From scarpèd cliff and quarried stone
> She cries, "A thousand types are gone;
> I care for nothing, all shall go."

Is this then to be the fate of man, who managed to believe in a God of love, though nature "red in tooth and claw" gave no evidence to support such belief? He concludes:

> What hope of answer or redress?
> Behind the veil, behind the veil.

These lines recall Goethe's idea, taken over by Carlyle, that nature can be for the wise the revealing garment of God, only to say that nature has now conclusively drawn the veil over God. The lines represent the low point of *In Memoriam*; they carry the problem raised by science to the point of impasse. Afterwards, the poet can only say "Peace; come away," thus introducing a group in which he consoles himself along lines that evade the issue of science, and which leads to the muted despair of the section on the Second Christmas.

The view of nature here is modern, in that the problems raised by the science of Tennyson's time are still with us, only more so. The universe seems even vaster, more dangerous and less hospitable than in the 1840's; our landings on the dead and ugly moon, our approaches to Mars and Venus, suggest the infinity of waste, of inanimate unconsciousness, that surrounds us. Tennyson also looks toward our century in his recognition that love cannot endure as a purely humanistic value, that the scientific view must inevitably reduce love to sex. In the section that ends the Lazarus group, he says that even if some voice could tell us from the grave that there is no life beyond it:

> Yet if some voice that man could trust
> Should murmur from the narrow house,
> "The cheeks drop in, the body bows;
> Man dies: nor is there hope in dust:"

might I not say that love still gives value to such life as we have on earth? No, the thought of perpetual geological change:

> The moanings of the homeless sea,
> The sound of streams that swift or slow
> Draw down Æonian hills, and sow
> The dust of continents to be;

the thought of inevitable oblivion must change love's "sweetness more and more, / Half-dead to know that [it] shall die" (xxxv). Without some conviction of its permanence, love must be devalued. That prediction has been amply fulfilled in our time.

Why then does *In Memoriam* not seem pressingly modern? Not only in its affirmations, but even in its doubts, the poem seems a bit old-fashioned. We can admire it, but with a certain amount of historical projection—as a poem of its time. Partly, there is the difference in idiom. Tennyson does not say, in the section I have been discussing, that love will turn into sex; he says it will take on its "coarsest Satyr-shape," it will turn into lust—and that is not the way we talk about sex nowadays. But the important thing is that the whole question of religion versus science has ceased to interest us. Most of us never had any faith to lose, and we do not *think* that the lack of religion has left a hole in our lives. As for those who really do believe, my impression is that they have long since given up any hope of reconciling their faith with scientific evidence. In this, of course, they are following Tennyson's main prescription, as well as Kierkegaard's (Teilhard de Chardin seems anachronistic in his present-day attempt to reconcile evolution and religion [7]).

Graham Hough, in his article of 1947, "The Natural Theology of *In Memoriam*," is more willing than T. S. Eliot to accept some of Tennyson's affirmations. Inasmuch as Tennyson "wishes to provide an answer in scientific terms," to reconcile religion and evolution by telling us we must evolve spiritually—"Move upward, working out the beast" (cxviii) and thus herald "the crowning race" (Epilogue)—inasmuch as Tennyson is doing that, Hough thinks he is merely "manufacturing a conclusion to the poem which will at least appear to draw the scattered threads together. . . . But the real answer, the one that really satisfied him, is not in those terms at all. It is a thoroughgoing subjectivism which does not meet the difficulties raised by science, but simply bypasses them." And Hough quotes the lines from section cxxiv that seem to offer the central theological answer:

If e'er when faith had fall'n asleep,
I heard a voice "believe no more"
And heard an ever-breaking shore
That tumbled in the Godless deep;

A warmth within the breast would melt
The freezing reason's colder part,
And like a man in wrath the heart
Stood up and answer'd "I have felt."

"This seems both honest and extremely moving," says Hough, "but it is this subjectivist attitude in 'In Memoriam' that has received the severest criticism." [8]

This so-called subjectivist answer—which Browning was also working out during these years in "Saul"—runs like this. If we *feel*, when we are feeling most deeply, that there is a loving God and the soul is immortal, then this feeling must correspond to an objective reality.

The wish, that of the living whole
No life may fail beyond the grave,
Derives it not from what we have
The likest God within the soul? (LV)

Coleridge had already lent philosophical support to this argument: "Throughout animated nature, of each characteristic organ and faculty there exists a pre-assurance, an instinctive and practical anticipation; and no pre-assurance common to a whole species does in any instance prove delusive." And Carlyle declared: "The evidence to me of God—and the only evidence—is the feeling I have, deep down in the very bottom of my heart, of right and truth and justice. . . . Whoever looks into himself must be aware that at the centre of things is a mysterious Demiurgos—who is God, and who cannot in the least be adequately spoken of in any human words." [9]

Tennyson's subjectivist answer, then, is not arbitrary; he arrived through personal experience at what was becoming the characteristic answer of the age. Tennyson's answer in scientific terms was also becoming characteristic of the age. Having in 1837 studied Lyell's *Principles of Geology* (1830–1833), Tennyson seems to have found an answer to its gloomy implications in the popularized science of Robert Chambers's *Vestiges of the Natural History of Creation* (1844). Chambers interprets evolution in terms of progress and as evidence of a benevolent Providence—a line Browning had already taken in *Paracelsus* (1835). In his doubts and answers, Tennyson like all great writers was able to help bring a new age into being by telling the present age what its preoccupations were. His answers helped provide the staple of liberal opinion during the 1850's and 60's. According to the dramatic action of *In Memoriam*, the answers are not there but have to be evolved. Hallam, it is true, had already worked out the answers; but Hallam, we are told, was ahead of his time, was even the herald of a higher race than ours.

The fact that Tennyson's answers are characteristic of the mid-Victorian age he helped bring into being makes them seem more dated than some of them—the subjectivist answer, or the suspicion that science's latest findings are not the last word—really are. If we abstract from *In Memoriam* the doubts and answers as ideas, then we must ask whether they are convincing. We know they *were* convincing—that Queen Victoria and George Eliot were representative of many, in that after their husbands' deaths they read *In Memoriam* along with the Bible for consolation. But to ask whether the abstracted ideas are *still* convincing is to treat *In Memoriam* as a tract for the times to which we can no longer subscribe.

There is, however, another way of approaching the poem, the way of literary criticism. The literary critic wants to know whether, taken as a poem of its age, *In Memoriam* can still be considered a great poem. And the proper question for him is not whether the doubts and affirmations, especially the affirmations, are convincing in themselves, but whether they are justified and sustained by the dramatic action and by the texture or undersong of emotion and imagery. The question, in other words, is whether the feeling is honest and, if it is, whether there is a sufficiently genuine shift of feeling to justify the finally affirmative movement of the thought. It is to this question that I shall now turn, in order to show that *In Memoriam* is a great poem and that it has a dynamic unity of thought and feeling dependent on a dialectical principle of growth of a single consciousness. The backtrackings, the changes of mood, style and levels of intensity, even the apparent contradictions, are all signs of the genuineness of the experience and coherent aspects of a single developing consciousness.

We have to study *In Memoriam* carefully from beginning to end to be struck by the remarkable coherence of a poem the art of which is to look like a diary. The coherence shows not only within the groups into which most of the sections fall, but also in the progress—what Tennyson called "the way of a soul"—through the groups.[10] The curious thing is that when we have understood this coherence, we realize that it derives from an epistemological sophistication that renders the affirmations more substantial than they seem in the abstract, and renders even the subjectivist answer less simply subjectivist.

About the genuineness of the grief projected in the poem, there is no disagreement. No one at all sensitive to poetry can fail to be moved by section VII in which the poet, after a sleepless night, compulsively creeps at daybreak to Hallam's door on Wimpole Street.

> Dark house, by which once more I stand
>   Here in the long unlovely street,
>   Doors, where my heart was used to beat
> So quickly, waiting for a hand,
>
> A hand that can be clasp'd no more—
>   Behold me, for I cannot sleep,

> And like a guilty thing I creep
> At earliest morning to the door.

> He is not here; but far away
> The noise of life begins again,
> And ghastly thro' the drizzling rain
> On the bald street breaks the blank day.

Ghosts are guilty spirits that cannot rest; and the poet, haunting the street, seems a ghost mourning a ghost. This is one of two themes that give texture or sensuous substantiality to *In Memoriam*. One is the theme of reciprocal death: the poet has died vicariously with Hallam. The other is the erotic theme of touching: "Doors, where my heart was used to beat / So quickly, waiting for a hand." The poet's heart, like a lover's, used to beat quickly as he anticipated clasping Hallam's hand; and his grief in these early sections is concentrated in a desire for physical contact. His grief is compared, to take only two examples, to that of a maiden whose fiancé has died (VI); and to that of a widower who on waking "moves his doubtful arms" only to feel that the place beside him in bed is empty (XIII). So fixated is the poet at this stage on Hallam's physical presence that if Hallam should step off the ship returning his corpse to England, and "Should strike a sudden hand in mind," the poet would "not feel it to be strange" (XIV).

This erotic theme carries in section XL adumbrations of an answer having to do with rebirth: the poet tries to look upon Hallam's departure as parents do when they send a bride off to enter "other realms of love" to produce children who will knit present to future. But alas the analogy will not hold; the bride, after all, comes back to visit,

> But thou and I have shaken hands,
> Till growing winters lay me low;
> My paths are in the fields I know
> And thine in undiscover'd lands.

Yet the last line suggests that Hallam's death may nevertheless serve some still undiscovered purpose; and, indeed, in the Epilogue we see that it has served, through the experience of the poem, to set Tennyson's and the reader's face toward the future. *In Memoriam* has dramatic validity just because the answers proposed early in the poem cannot be sustained until the poet has himself undergone a total revolution in perception.

The theme of reciprocal death carries its adumbrations of an answer when Tennyson, standing at Hallam's burial, thinks of resuscitating him according to the prophet Elisha's method—by breathing into Hallam's mouth the last breath of his own almost expiring life.

> Ah yet, ev'n yet, if this might be,
> I, falling on his faithful heart,
> Would breathing thro' his lips impart
> The life that almost dies in me;

but no, it is the expiring Tennyson who will have to be resuscitated by the dead Hallam:

> That dies not, but endures with pain,
> And slowly forms the firmer mind,
> Treasuring the look it cannot find,
> The words that are not heard again.
>   (xviii)

Resuscitation or rebirth means learning to accept Hallam's death.

The theme of reciprocal death leads into the question of religion. For "the Shadow fear'd of man," who broke our physical contact and rendered formless the image of you that gave life form for me, "spread his mantle dark and cold, / And wrapt thee formless in the fold." Somewhere in the formless waste, that "Shadow sits and waits for me" (xxii); and is "The Shadow cloak'd from head to foot, / Who keeps the keys of all the creeds" (xxiii)—the creeds that try to give life form.

The theme of reciprocal death leads also to the first statement of the question of nature. In section II, the yew is addressed as symbolizing the death principle in nature, a principle into which the poet feels utterly absorbed: "I seem to fail from out my blood / And grow incorporate into thee." Out of this mood, Sorrow in the next section whispers that the stars blindly run. But this scientific truth is whispered from Sorrow's "lying lip" and in the last stanza the poet resists Sorrow's view of the world, calling her a blind thing.

> And shall I take a thing so blind,
> Embrace her as my natural good;
> Or crush her, like a vice of blood,
> Upon the threshold of the mind?

"Vice of blood" connects with "I seem to fail from out my blood," suggesting that Sorrow's view of nature emerges from the death instinct inside us, and is therefore as much a pathetic fallacy as the view of nature that emerges from the Wordsworthian sense of joy. Even in the climactic statements of the nature question, the views of nature as "careless of the single life" and "red in tooth and claw" are presented as "evil dreams" (LV, LVI). But in the preceding section, the opposite view of nature—"Oh yet we trust that somehow good / Will be the final goal of ill, / . . . That not a worm is cloven in vain"—is summed up: "So runs my dream." The oscillation belongs to the strategy of realism and sincerity at the heart of In Memoriam. But it reflects also an epistemological sophistication that provides the dramatic action and the adumbrations of an answer. For the poet, when he dies vicariously with Hallam, has to admit into his mind, though he struggles against it, the view of nature as purposelessly destructive. But the struggle signifies a contrary movement toward the internal change that will transform Hallam's death into a life-enhancing force and will enable the poet to see the very same facts as having quite a different meaning.

A group of metaphysical speculations on the state of the soul

after death suggests that we are reborn into this world and the
next, and that we evolve in this world the self that can be reborn
in the next (XLIV, XLV). But it is the "lying" Sorrow of section III
who now tries to comfort us with such fancies (XLVIII); and such
fancies are mere ripples on the deep pool of the poet's grief
(XLIX). The final answer will have to emerge from the depths, and
we are therefore returned to the deep grief of:

> Be near me when my light is low,
>   When the blood creeps, and the nerves prick
>   And tingle; and the heart is sick,
>   And all the wheels of Being slow,   (L)

which leads to the climactic statement of the nature question.

There follows a group offering conceits (the superficiality is dramatically right) on Hallam in heaven and a group on consolatory
dreams—all of which show the poet moving toward surface cheer-
fulness though deep down the grief remains. The grief, however,
rushes back to the surface in the powerful section LXXII, where the
stormy first anniversary of Hallam's death reminds the poet of the
day he received the devastating news. The grief increases as he
thinks in the next two sections of the fame Hallam would have
had and says, in the next three, that he can only write these verses
for his own relief though he knows they will not endure or have
any effect. (Throughout, there are enough references to pastoral
motifs to remind us that the pastoral elegy has been abandoned in
the interest of realism and sincerity, and that the traditional
themes of pastoral elegy are reversed: nature does not mourn the
dead man, who will not have fame and will not be immortalized
by this poem.) All these sections help define the quality of the
grief by the time of the second Christmas—when grief's "deep relations are the same, / But with long use her tears are dry"
(LXXVIII).

The three Christmases, which stand for almost seventeen years,
are the most obvious markers of spiritual development. In the dull

group immediately following the second Christmas (the only really uninteresting group in the poem), there are two sections that seem extraneous but are there, I think, to fill out the general scheme. In one, the poet declares his love for his favorite brother, Charles, even though he has written of Hallam: "More than my brothers are to me" (LXXIX); in the other, the poet offers to Edmund Lushington a friendship that will substitute in his heart for Hallam's though it cannot be as intense (LXXXV). Both sections show the poet turning back to life, realizing that Hallam can be fulfilled through living men. This prepares us for the Epilogue in which Hallam will be reborn through Lushington's wedding with one of Tennyson's sisters (Hallam had been engaged to another); for the child of this marriage will make a link to that future from which Hallam, as herald of "the crowning race," beckons. It is right that the Epilogue descends to domestic life, where the sublime principle of Love perceived in the closing sections, must be made operative.

But the turning to Charles and Lushington is only preparatory. The next magnificent group leads to the real turning point of *In Memoriam*, section XCV, where in a mystical trance the poet has the epiphany that transforms and transcends all the problems of the poem. I am inclined to start this group with the charmingly poignant section LXXXVII, where the poet, on a visit to Hallam's rooms at Cambridge, makes the last important revival of Hallam as a vital individual; Hallam is from now on to be revived through diffusion into forms other than his bodily form. The group in any case starts with the next very beautiful section, in which the wild bird's song is understood as combining opposites through total vision—"The glory of the sum of things"—which adumbrates the final answer of the group and the poem.

> Wild bird, whose warble, liquid sweet,
> Rings Eden thro' the budded quicks,
> O tell me where the senses mix,
> O tell me where the passions meet,

> Whence radiate: fierce extremes employ
> Thy spirits in the darkening leaf,
> And in the midmost heart of grief
> Thy passion clasps a secret joy.

Just as the bird's answer to grief is beyond its own understanding; so the poet hopes that even if his harp begins with woe, some force beyond his understanding ("I cannot all command the strings") will take over, so that:

> The glory of the sum of things
> Will flash along the chords and go.

There emerges again the question of Hallam's revival. Come in spring in your bodily form, says the poet, but in summer:

> Come, beauteous in thine after form,
> And like a finer light in light.   (xci)

And in section xcii—which parallels section xiv where we were told that if Hallam stepped off the ship alive, the poet would not think it strange—in section xcii, we are told that if a vision should reveal Hallam in his bodily form, and even if Hallam spoke prophecies that came true, the poet would understand the experience as only the action of his own mind. The poet now locates spiritual reality in his own consciousness. "I shall not see thee," he says in the next section, but long to meet

> Where all the nerve of sense is numb,
> Spirit to Spirit, Ghost to Ghost,

but to achieve such communion with the dead, one's spirit must be like theirs "at peace with all" (xciv). At the opening of section xcv, where the communion takes place, the poet is at peace, and he learns to be "at peace with all."

Section xcv is constructed like a Wordsworthian dramatic lyric, in that the thought develops out of and as a counterpart to the natural setting. "By night we linger'd on the lawn." The Tennysons are gathered outside their house at Somersby, during one of those long hushed English summer twilights in which things remain half-visible:

> and o'er the sky
> The silvery haze of summer drawn;

> And calm that let the tapers burn
> Unwavering: not a cricket chirr'd:
> The brook alone far-off was heard,
> And on the board the fluttering urn:

> And bats went round in fragrant skies,
> And wheel'd or lit the filmy shapes
> That haunt the dusk . . .

> . . .

> While now we sang old songs that peal'd
> From knoll to knoll, where, couch'd at ease,
> The white kine glimmer'd, and the trees
> Laid their dark arms about the field.

When the others withdraw, "A hunger seized my heart," and he reads Hallam's letters—finding in them "love's dumb cry defying change" and Hallam's ability to look through doubts and "wordy snares" to the positive "suggestion" behind them. Like the wild bird's song, the letters turn negation into affirmation; their words turn into an epiphany, a manifestation of Hallam's living soul.

> The living soul was flash'd on mine,

> And mine in this was wound, and whirl'd
> About empyreal heights of thought,
> And came on that which is, and caught
> The deep pulsations of the world,

> Æonian music measuring out
> The steps of Time—the shocks of Chance—
> The blows of Death.

The epiphany reveals "The glory of the sum of things"; it is a vision of process, turning the geological aeons into "Æonian music." "With the flash of a trembling glance," says St. Augustine in the *Confessions*, the mind "arrived at *that which is.*" [11]

When the trance is over, doubt returns and we are returned to the same landscape:

> Till now the doubtful dusk reveal'd
> The knolls once more where, couch'd at ease,
> The white kine glimmer'd. . . .

But the landscape is not the same. For "suck'd from out the distant gloom / A breeze"—Wordsworth's "correspondent breeze," corresponding to inner rebirth—now animates the trees and flowers, saying:

> "The dawn, the dawn," and died away;
> And East and West, without a breath,
> Mixt their dim lights, like life and death,
> To broaden into boundless day.

The breeze shows that the epiphany has transformed the poet's perception, even if he can now only reflect upon the epiphany through inadequate forms of speech and thought. The climactic counterpart to the internal transformation is the transformation of the doubtful twilight dusk into the doubtful dusk of dawn. The glimmering white kine seem to symbolize the Truth that can be apprehended only through doubtful dusks; while the two dusks, which seem in the short Northern summer night to mix into each other, are in the boundless light of Eternity seen, as like life and death, two necessary aspects of a single reality.

Graham Hough defines three major elements in *In Memoriam* —the influence of science, the influence of Coleridge to which I would add the influence of Wordsworth and Carlyle, and Tenny-

son's own religious intuitions based on his capacity since childhood to experience mystical trances. Hough finds these elements
"not completely unified and the balance between them . . .
unstable." [12] I would suggest that these elements are unified according to a scheme showing what I have called Tennyson's epistemological sophistication. For In Memoriam is organized to show
that after the poet has undergone a total transformation of perception, all the old facts and problems are transvaluated and absorbed
into the affirmative movement that dominates the poem from section xcv on.

In section xcvi, the doubt Hallam engaged in is shown to be a
religious virtue: Moses on Sinai stood "in the darkness and the
cloud," whereas the Israelites below insisted on seeing "their gods
of gold." The second anniversary of Hallam's death brings consolation through his diffusion in, and assimilation to, the natural cycle.
But the Tennysons are to move from Somersby and the landscape
associated with Hallam. This problem is resolved in the important
section ciii, which restates allegorically the resolution of section
xcv. The poet had a dream of the dead from which he woke—a
sign of how far we have come—"content." He saw in his dream a
"statue veil'd" round which maidens sang; and though he recognized "The shape of him I loved," the veil and the word "shape"
suggest that Hallam has transcended his earthly identity. The
maidens wept but accompanied the poet, as he sailed in a little
boat down a river, overhung with vegetation, into an ocean—
where he felt himself growing bigger, stronger, more masculine,
and where on a great ship they saw the "man we loved" but
"thrice as large as man." The poet's growth in size is a sign that
he has grown in perception to the point where he can now see
Hallam as superhuman. "Up the side I went / And fell in silence
on his neck." The maidens wept, thinking they were to be left behind; but Hallam bade them enter in, and they all sail away from
shore toward "a crimson cloud" that is like another shore. Clearly,
Hallam is no longer to be tied to a physical image or location; his

death, in this new realm of value, turns into a positive good. The maidens can be understood as the melancholy, backward-looking, feminine, erotic muses of the earlier sections, which are in the boundless ocean, the poet's trip from sensuous to transcendental perception, subsumed into the masculine, affirmative, forward-looking muses of the concluding section.[13]

This spiritual development is marked by the third Christmas on which the Tennysons, now removed from Somersby, break entirely with the past—with "grief" that abuses "the genial hour," even with old Christmas customs—and turn their thoughts to the future: "The closing cycle rich in good" (cv). Instead of the vegetation cycle that offered consolation in the old elegies, we now have Hallam's faith in progress. That is why, in the next three sections, the New Year bells are asked to "Ring out the darkness of the land, / Ring in the Christ that is to be"; Hallam's birthday can be celebrated with "festal cheer"; and the poet declares: I will no longer "eat my heart alone," but turn my private sorrow into compassion for humanity. There is a diffusion, which Hallam would approve, of values originally concentrated in Hallam.

A new group characterizes Hallam as he was in life, with greater detail and poignancy than before. The purpose is to recall by implication the elegiac theme, "Alas, he is dead," in order to return with even stronger affirmations—the affirmations discussed earlier in this essay. But the affirmations have not, as I have tried to show, been plucked out of the blue. They have been prepared from the start by a submerged counter-movement of the instincts, that offered all along adumbrations of an answer, and led finally to the total revolution in perception that has given to the same facts a different meaning. We can see this through certain deliberately planted parallels. Section cxix parallels section vii on Wimpole Street. Again, the poet stands at daybreak before Hallam's door. but this time "not as one that weeps"; for he no longer needs the physical pressure of Hallam's hand, it is enough that "in my thoughts with scarce a sigh / I take the pressure of thine hand." [14]

In the lovely section cxxi, "Sad Hesper," the evening star, is blended with the morning star, "Bright Phosphor" to make "Sweet Hesper-Phosphor, double name"—in the manner of the wild bird's song and the blending of twilight and dawn in section xcv. The epiphany of section xcv is alluded to in section cxxii, which parallels the moving pessimism of section l: "Be near me when my light is low." In section cxxii, the poet now asks Hallam: were you with me in that moment of vision when I understood the unity of all things?

> Oh, wast thou with me, dearest, then,
>   While I rose up against my doom,
>   And yearn'd to burst the folded gloom,
> To bare the eternal Heavens again,
>
> To feel once more, in placid awe,
>   The strong imagination roll
>   A sphere of stars about my soul,
> In all her motion one with law;
>
> If thou wert with me, and the grave
>   Divide us not, be with me now,

transform my thoughts, turn grief into joy, so that "As in the former flash of joy," the epiphany of section xcv, "I slip the thoughts of life and death," and "every thought breaks out a rose."

Thus, Lyell's geology is transformed into a gorgeous poetic vision of earth's fluidity, perhaps the most beautiful rendition in English poetry of a modern scientific theory.

> There rolls the deep where grew the tree.
>   O earth, what changes hast thou seen!
>   There where the long street roars, hath been
> The stillness of the central sea.
>
> The hills are shadows, and they flow
>   From form to form, and nothing stands;

> They melt like mist, the solid lands,
> Like clouds they shape themselves and go.

The last stanza seems to stand in simple opposition to these two:

> But in my spirit will I dwell,
> And dream my dream, and hold it true;
> For tho' my lips may breathe adieu,
> I cannot think the thing farewell. (cxxiii)

But the point is, as in Hopkins's "Pied Beauty," that when one sees change as beautiful, one is seeing through to a principle of permanence behind change.

The point is reasserted in the next section after a restatement both of the problem—that the principle of permanence, God, cannot be found either in nature or through reason—and the solution:

> like a man in wrath the heart
> Stood up and answer'd, "I have felt."

An earlier subjectivist assertion of this sort was dismissed:

> So runs my dream: but what am I?
> An infant crying in the night. (liv)

Now the assertion is sustained. "No," says the poet, I did not answer like a man in wrath but "like a child in doubt and fear." Yet "that blind clamour made me wise"; I was like a child that "crying, knows his father near." Crying made real the thing I was crying for; it taught me what I truly am. And when "what I [truly] am beheld again / What is, and no man understands," then

> out of darkness came the hands
> That reach thro' nature, moulding men. (cxxiv)

Hallam's *hand* has been transformed into mystical *hands*.

In other words, the assertion "I have felt" is not so simple-mindedly subjectivist as it seems in isolation. For it is not made against an unyielding reality, but against a reality that the beholder has transformed. The transformation has validity to the extent that the beholder has reached a state of perception that brings to the surface his deepest instincts (the poet says in section cxxv that instinctive Hope and Love were never absent from his song) —instincts which, when they are deep enough, connect with external reality. Thus, internal and external reality are connected through the love of Hallam. The poet must have a personal, which is to say a genuine, experience of love and value to be able to diffuse love and value throughout nature and society, and thus restore the sense of nature's life and the sense of connection with the rest of the world, which Hallam's death killed in him. As the poet works this restoration, he finds he can answer those early nineteenth-century scientific theories that rationalized for him his own despair; and he finds he can reinforce the transcendental philosophies of Coleridge and Carlyle which rationalize his new mood of affirmation.

No wonder Tennyson got the idea, as he organized *In Memoriam*, of modeling his poem on the *Divine Comedy*. For in Dante, too, it is a personal experience, love of Beatrice in life, that leads to a diffusion of value—to the love of Beatrice in death that leads in turn to visions of the Virgin and God. And Dante, too, used the available science and philosophy to help create the world-view of his time by envisioning it. In section cxxx, the sense that the spirit of Hallam lives in nature blends, through a principle of love, with the sense that God lives in nature.

> Thy voice is on the rolling air;
> I hear thee where the waters run;
> Thou standest in the rising sun,
> And in the setting thou art fair.
>
> What art thou then? I cannot guess;
> But tho' I seem in star and flower

To feel thee some diffusive power,
I do not therefore love thee less!

My love involves the love before;
My love is vaster passion now;
Tho' mixed with God and Nature thou,
I seem to love thee more and more.

And in the last numbered section (cxxxi), which is pure prayer,
I hear the echo of Dante's last passage in *Paradiso*. (Hallam vener-
ated Dante, especially his *Paradiso*.) Dante's intellect retreats before the direct Vision of God, which is beyond his understanding.
But he discovers through his deepest instincts, his own desire and
will, the desire and will that roll through all things and move the
visible universe. "Here imagination failed," says Dante, "but already my desire and will were rolled. . . ." Tennyson begins:

O LIVING will that shalt endure
When all that seems shall suffer shock,
Rise in the spiritual rock,
Flow thro' our deeds and make them pure,

That we may lift from out of dust
A voice as unto him that hears,

that we may pray *as though* God exists. There is still the equivoca-
tion characteristic of Tennyson's theology. But Tennyson explained "O living will" as referring to individual free will that
connects with Divine Will and the visible universe. Free will was,
he said, the "main miracle, apparently an act of self-limitation by
the Infinite, and yet a revelation by Himself of Himself." [15] The
last stanza shows the influence of Carlyle and of Hallam's "Theo-
dicaea Novissima" based on love:

With faith that comes of self-control,
The truths that never can be proved
Until we close with all we loved,
And all we flow from, soul in soul.

But those last two lines reflect Dante's discovery that his own desire and will were blended (as in Tennyson's "O living will") with God's:

> but already
> my desire and will were rolled—as a wheel
> that is turned evenly—by the Love that moves
> the sun and the other stars.[16]

Dante's discovery led back, we know, to an established and public theology. But Tennyson, too, makes connection with the developing liberal or Broad Church theology of F. D. Maurice and others. Eleanor Mattes speaks of Maurice's influence on the Prologue, dated 1849, which is apparently Christian, but still relativist:

> Our little systems have their day;
> They have their day and cease to be:
> They are but broken lights of thee,
> And thou, O Lord, art more than they.

But Tennyson's faith beyond the forms of faith has still wider application, in that it remains the unstated eclectic religion of liberals who are even vaguely theistic—though we allude to our faith in new terms, terms borrowed from depth psychology and anthropology. Among church members, too, Tennyson's faith informs the new ecumenical spirit which recognizes all creeds as possible responses to an ultimate reality that can be experienced but not known. What matters for such a faith—as it matters for gauging the success of *In Memoriam*—is not the creed but its undersong or symbolic texture, and that the creed really be arrived at through a process of personal discovery.

BROWNING
AND
THE QUESTION
OF MYTH

The history of criticism is largely the history of the changing questions we ask about works of art. The pre-eminence in our time of Yeats, Eliot and Joyce, and the connection of these writers with an artistic method and a mode of thought that Eliot, in reviewing Joyce's *Ulysses*, has himself called *mythical*—all this leads me to ask about Browning's use of myth. The question seems particularly relevant since Yeats and Browning had in common an intense admiration for Shelley. Now Yeats, we know, admired not Shelley the Godwinian radical, but Shelley the Platonist and mythmaker —the Shelley who, in the manner of Blake, used archetypal symbols.[1] The question is whether Browning—who did for a time admire Shelley the Godwinian radical—had affinities also with Shelley the mythmaker and (the two terms are inextricably connected) symbolist.

It is certainly the visionary whom Browning praises in the essay he wrote on Shelley in 1852. "I would rather consider Shelley's poetry as a sublime fragmentary essay towards a presentment of the correspondency of the universe to Deity, of the natural to the spiritual, and of the actual to the ideal, than I would isolate and sepa-

76

rately appraise the worth of many detachable portions which might be acknowledged as utterly perfect in a lower moral point of view, under the mere conditions of art." Shelley's main excellence is "his simultaneous perception of Power and Love in the absolute, and of Beauty and Good in the concrete, while he throws, from his poet's station between both, swifter, subtler, and more numerous films for the connection of each with each, than have been thrown by any modern artificer of whom I have knowledge; proving how, as he says,—'The spirit of the worm within the sod / In love and worship blends itself with God.' " [2]

Those lines might have been written by Blake—a sign that Browning comes in this passage very close to Yeats's appreciation of Shelley in terms applicable to a mythmaking poet like Blake. Browning offers, in defining Shelley's main excellence, a good definition of the myth-making poet—of the poet who does not merely make decorative allusions to an established literary mythology, but who actually *sees* the world as mythical, who sees man, nature, and God as intimately engaged in a natural-supernatural story.

To ask about Browning's use of myth is to ask two questions. The first is whether Browning believed in using—as Arnold did in *Sohrab* and *Merope*, and Tennyson did in the *Idylls*—the grand old enduring subjects that have come down to us in the literary tradition. The answer to the first question is no. Browning agreed with Miss Barrett, when she said in that often-quoted letter to him: "I am inclined to think that we want new *forms*, as well as thoughts. The old gods are dethroned. Why should we go back to the antique moulds, classical moulds, as they are so improperly called?" [3] Browning himself said as much and more when, at the end of his life, he dealt, in "Parleying With Gerard de Lairesse," with the question of how far the Greeks ought to be used as models for modern art. We have gone beyond the Greeks, he concluded, in religion and in moral and psychological insight. Modern poets should not, therefore, pour new wine into old bottles. They should no longer

"Dream afresh old godlike shapes,
Recapture ancient fable that escapes,
Push back reality, repeople earth
With vanished falseness, recognize no worth
In fact new-born unless 't is rendered back
Pallid by fancy, as the western rack
Of fading cloud bequeaths the lake some gleam
Of its gone glory!"   (382–389)

We should not ignore reality in favor of old subjects from mythology. Nor should we render modern facts poetical by decorating them with outworn mythological allusions.

On the issue raised by Arnold in the Preface to his *Poems* of 1853—the issue as to which subjects are better for modern poetry, the grand, enduring subjects or subjects drawn from modern life—Browning stood against Arnold and with the modern realists.[4] It is true that Browning himself almost always used subjects drawn from the past. But he used them as history rather than myth. This explains his taste for little-known characters and incidents out of the past. For such characters and incidents have clearly not come down to us through the literary tradition. We can believe in the factuality of characters and incidents whose existence is authenticated even though they are no longer remembered. The forgotten historical character is the very opposite of the mythical character whose historical existence is doubtful even though he is vividly 'remembered.'

The historical attitude suggests that the past was as confused and unglamorous as the present. The historical attitude is also interested in tracing change—in showing how different were the ideas and values of the past from ours, in showing that the past was itself in the process of change. Yet the historical change is apparent because we can measure it against a recognizably continuous human or psychological reality. This again is opposite to the mythical attitude, which idealizes the past in order to set it up as a permanent criterion of value. At the same time, the mythical attitude makes the people of the past seem different from us, larger, sometimes superhuman. It is the past as permanent criterion that Arnold had in mind in the Preface. In his very use of the past, then, Browning disagreed with Arnold. And he disagreed, too, on that other important issue of the Preface—Arnold's attack on internal drama, on the idea that modern poetry ought to treat, in Browning's phrase, "the incidents in the development of a soul."

On the issues raised by Arnold in the Preface and elsewhere, Browning was mainly right. For it is surely a weakness in Arnold's critical position that, while he could see art as dependent on the power of both the man and the moment, he should have supposed that the masterwork of one historical moment could or should have the virtues of the masterwork of another historical moment. Browning, on the other hand, was wrong in not understanding the importance of an action or of some external mechanism for portraying an internal state. Browning's poems fail just to the extent that his characters describe and analyze their thoughts and emotions, without any vividly apparent external reason for doing so. Browning was interested in talking about both history and psychology, and his problem as an artist was to find a means for doing so. Now a *mythos* or action, properly understood, is a way of accomplishing this end. For the kind of action we call mythical, just because it does not imitate a strictly external reality, is the kind that can speak with one voice of both internal and external reality. The problem is to use myth or the mythical method without archaizing —to use them in a distinctively modern way.

We have here a criterion for understanding the course of Browning's development and for assessing his work. For while he failed in *Paracelsus* and *Sordello* to reconcile internal and external reality, the two are successfully brought together in the best dramatic monologues. In *Paracelsus,* Browning fails because he has pushed offstage just those historical events that might have given outline and interest to his obscure historical character. What we get through a long poem is a continuing high-pitched reaction to we hardly know what; and we find ourselves longing for those vulgar events that Browning was so proud to have excluded.

In his long labors over *Sordello*, however, Browning apparently wrestled with the problem of reconciling internal and external reality. As DeVane has shown in his *Browning Handbook*, *Sordello* was written in four different periods, in each of which Browning took a quite different view of his subject. In the first version, Browning treated his obscure historical character in the manner of *Paracelsus*—he gave us the history of a soul. In the second version, he made Sordello a man of action, a warrior and lover, thus showing Sordello's impact on the world around him. In the third version, he neglected Sordello himself and concentrated on the historical events of the period. In the fourth version, he rounded out his plot by making Sordello the champion of the masses and Salinguerra's son. The four Sordellos, which are imposed one upon the other, never do add up to a single *Sordello*.

It is just the elements of the first three *Sordellos* that are brought together in the best dramatic monologues. They are not brought together by plot—if by plot we mean a complete action, the kind that ties all the threads together and therefore seems to modern writers, especially novelists, who judge by the criteria of realism, to offer too neat a rationalization of the material. But the three elements are nonetheless brought together by an action—a direction of the speaker's energies outward. It is because the speaker is not trying to tell the truth about himself, but is trying to accomplish something or make an impression, that he actually does reveal himself truly. This is the way characters reveal themselves in drama.

As in drama, the speaker has outline because we see him not, as we see Paracelsus, in a confiding relation; we see him rather in a conflicting relation with another person. And we get, therefore, through the contrast, a sense of how he looks from the outside. The speaker also has outline because his fundamental human energies are clothed in the predilections peculiar to his age—as in "The Bishop Orders His Tomb," where the Italian Renaissance bishop manifests his competitiveness and desire for immortality by ordering for himself a more expensive tomb than his rival's. A whole way of seeing, thinking and feeling is manifested through that aim; so that we get through one action the man and the age, the man as he looks to others and himself, the outer and the inner reality. The action is, however, incomplete. That is the price Browning pays for using a realistic action; for the characteristically realistic action is the slice-of-life.

His best dramatic monologues entitle Browning to his rank among the two or three best Victorian poets. But is he also—as he certainly aimed to be—one of the great poets of English literature? In trying to answer, we have to admit that even in his best volume, *Men and Women*, Browning was tempted—in dramatic monologues like "Cleon" and "Bishop Blougram"—to slip back to the analytic, discursive style of the earlier, the *Paracelsus* period. And we know how, in the later dramatic monologues—in "Mr. Sludge," "Prince Hohenstiel-Schwangau," "Fifine"—he did slip back, without even the lyric fire of the *Paracelsus* period.

We have also to admit that even his very best dramatic monologues remain, after all, only splendid vignettes—"prismatic hues," as he himself called them. They do not add up to what Browning called "the pure white light,".[5] the total vision of life that the greatest poets give us, and that Browning from the start—from the time of *Sordello*—intended to give us. *The Ring and the Book*, of course, is Browning's climactic attempt to give us a total vision of life. He brings several dramatic monologues, several points of view together, in order to collapse the "prismatic hues" into "the pure white light"—in order to make explicit what is implicit in all the dramatic monologues, that the relative is an index to the absolute, that the relative is our way of apprehending the absolute.

This brings us to the second question about Browning's use of myth, the question that arises from our experience of Yeats, Eliot and Joyce. In reviewing *Ulysses* for *The Dial* of November 1923,

Eliot argues that Joyce is not as people think a "prophet of chaos," but that he has given us the materials of modern disorder and shown us how to impose order upon them. He has done this by what Eliot calls "the mythical method." Eliot is referring to the continuous parallel between the trivial and apparently meaningless events of Joyce's novel and the events in the *Odyssey*.

> In using the myth, in manipulating a continuous parallel between contemporaneity and antiquity, Mr. Joyce is pursuing a method which others must pursue after him. . . . It is simply a way of controlling, of ordering, of giving a shape and a significance to the immense panorama of futility and anarchy which is contemporary history. It is a method already adumbrated by Mr. Yeats. . . . It is a method for which the horoscope is auspicious. Psychology . . . ethnology [i.e., anthropology], and *The Golden Bough* have concurred to make possible what was impossible even a few years ago. Instead of narrative method, we may now use the mythical method. It is, I seriously believe, a step toward making the modern world possible for art, toward . . . order and form.

With the mythical method, the modern writer can render the disordered surface of modern life, while showing how nevertheless the mythical patterns inevitably reassert themselves at the unconscious roots of existence. This is the method Eliot himself uses in *The Waste Land*.

Now the whole point of *The Ring and the Book* was to pull out of a forgotten and sordid old Roman murder case the Christian scheme of sin and redemption. Having himself, in an experience of illumination, seen through to the *truth* of the case, Browning's artistic strategy for conveying that truth was to restore *The Old Yellow Book* in which he had found the documents of the case. He wanted to give us the experience of reading the raw documents, to give us the jumbled real-life surface of the case and yet make us see through the facts—the facts so peculiar to the place and time—an eternal pattern. This is something like what Eliot says Joyce does.

Something, but not quite. For the case, as Browning renders it, does not really present a surface of ambivalence; and the pattern is rather too explicitly a moral pattern. We feel, as a result, that we are getting not absolute truth, but Browning's notions about absolute truth. *The Ring and the Book*, therefore, in spite of the many great things in it, does not in the end quite come off. Browning is more convincing in the best dramatic monologues, where he gives us truth as simply a relative manifestation that points somehow to the absolute. How? Through the fundamental human energy of the speaker, that seems to lead back to an unconscious ground of existence where all energies merge and are justified.

It is out of this unconscious ground that myths, according to twentieth-century theory, arise.[6] And there remains, in *The Ring and the Book*, a pattern which is in Eliot's sense mythical because underlying. I mean the pattern of the Andromeda-Perseus myth and its Christian analogue, the myth of St. George and the dragon. We know that Browning's imagination was dominated throughout his career by the image of the beautiful Andromeda, chained naked to the rock, waiting helplessly for the serpent to come out of the sea to devour her, but waiting also—though she does not consciously know this—for Perseus to descend miraculously—to "come," as Browning puts it in *Pauline*, "in thunder from the stars"—to rescue her. The combination of sexual and spiritual ramifications gives the image its strength and validity.

The Andromeda-St George myth connected Browning's life and art, giving him, as only myths can, what Yeats called Unity of Being. In the greatest event of his life, he repeated the mythical pattern by rescuing Miss Barrett. And there is no doubt that he recognized the same mythical pattern when he read in *The Old Yellow Book* about Caponsacchi's rescue of Pompilia. He even changed the date of the rescue to make it fall on St. George's Day. It was because Browning was able to assimilate the murder case to the myth that *The Ring and the Book* is at once a very personal and a very impersonal poem.

There are many references throughout *The Ring and the Book* to the Andromeda-St. George myth, and it is used rather as the vegetation myth is used in *The Waste Land*. We are made to see a continuity between the pagan and Christian versions of the same myth. And all the characters seem inevitably to have some memory of the myth—though the debased characters remember it in a debased form; while the cynical characters, who see Caponsacchi's rescue as an abduction, turn the myth into its obverse, the myth of Helen and Paris.[7] Nevertheless, the references remain only references—mythological allusions to illustrate points that are really being made discursively.

The Ring and the Book is an important poem, because it moves in the right direction. It moves away from myth as overt subject matter; yet it goes so far as to bring back the mythical pattern— not the particular events and characters of the Andromeda story, but the pattern—as inherent in the very structure of the mind, in what we would nowadays call the unconscious. *The Ring and the Book* does the same thing for the Christian pattern of sin and redemption—bringing Christian virtue alive again out of what Miss Barrett, in the letter I have quoted, calls "this low ground," and through circumstances, like Caponsacchi's abduction of Pompilia, which would seem the reverse of virtuous. The fact that Miss Barrett goes on, after inveighing against subjects drawn from classical mythology, to say that "Christianity is a worthy *myth*, and poetically acceptable," [8] shows that she and Browning were against the classical mythology of the official literary tradition, because it projects obsolete meanings we only pretend to believe in as a literary game. It is because Browning did not go far enough in his use of mythical pattern, did not allow the meaning of his poem to rest in the pattern, that he considered that myths could grow obsolete.

Browning's idea of progress would seem to prevent a complete reliance on mythical pattern. For Yeats, the symbols and myths are permanent, and the ideas about them change. But for Browning, the myths change; myths are the progressively changing symbolic language for the same continuing idea. In "Parleying With

Charles Avison," Browning takes off from the idea, expressed forty years earlier in a letter to Miss Barrett, that " 'in Music, the Beau Idéal changes every thirty years.' " [9] Music, like Avison's, of a generation or two ago, seems so obsolete; yet the thing music talks about remains the same, and it requires only a few technical adjustments to translate from an old to a new musical idiom. We need the ever-changing idioms to startle us over and over again into ever new apprehensions of the old truth. For "Truths escape / Time's insufficient garniture: they fade, / They fall"—when the old garniture seems to turn into a lie. In the same way,

> Soon shall fade and fall
> Myth after myth—the husk-like lies I call
> New truth's corolla-safeguard.
> (371–373, 378–380)

Certainly, the mythical method as practiced by Yeats, Eliot and Joyce depends on an idea of recurrence, on a cyclical rather than a linear view of history.[10] The idea of progress requires that you keep track of time; while the mythical method requires that you collapse time. Browning does collapse time whenever he writes about Andromeda, and it is significant that he always writes well on that subject. The Andromeda passage in his first poem, *Pauline* (656 667), is one of the finest passages he ever wrote. The passage is quite remarkably echoed by Hopkins's "Andromeda" sonnet.

I mention the similarity to suggest that Hopkins, in spite of the many nasty things he said about Browning (things that show a minute knowledge of the older poet's work), must to some extent have learned his music from Browning. Both poets are obscure because they are trying to use words in such a way as to overcome the analytic effect of language—the effect Browning has in mind when he talks about Sordello's failure to create a satisfactory poetic language,

> Because perceptions whole, like that he sought
> To clothe, reject so pure a work of thought

As language: thought may take perception's place
But hardly co-exist in any case,
Being its mere presentment—of the whole
By parts, the simultaneous and the sole
By the successive and the many.   (589–595)

The crowd, Browning goes on to say, which deals in ready-made thoughts, has merely to tack them together; and presumably the crowd can be lucid. But for Sordello, thought and language are the things perception has been rent into. They are the diffusion and destruction of perception; and it is the point of poetic language to give that sense of itself.[11] Both Browning and Hopkins break up conventional syntax and multiply associations with bewildering rapidity, in order to make us feel that the things language has laid out in space and time and in an order of succession are really happening simultaneously—in order to restore the instantaneous, orchestrated quality of the original perception. Both poets are working for an effect characteristic of symbolism and the mythical method.

In defending himself in a letter to Ruskin against Ruskin's charge of obscurity, Browning explains that the poetry or effect of simultaneity lies precisely in the jumps that the reader is forced to make for himself.

> I *know* that I don't make out my conception by my language, all poetry being a putting the infinite within the finite. You would have me paint it all plain out, which can't be; but by various artifices I try to make shift with touches and bits of outlines which *succeed* if they bear the conception from me to you. You ought, I think, to keep pace with the thought tripping from ledge to ledge of my "glaciers," as you call them; not stand poking your alpenstock into the holes, and demonstrating that no foot could have stood there;—suppose it sprang over there? In *prose* you may criticise so—because that is the absolute representation of portions of truth, what chronicling is to history—but in asking for more *ultimates* you must accept less *mediates,* nor expect that a Druid stone-circle will be traced

> for you with as few breaks to the eye as the North Crescent
> and South Crescent that go together so cleverly in many a
> suburb.

And he says of a poem of his: "Is the jump too much there? The whole is all but a simultaneous feeling with me." [12]

Browning sketches out what has come to be the dominant twentieth-century theory about poetry—that it makes its effect through the association in the reader's mind of disparate elements, and that this process of association leads to the recognition, in what has been presented successively, of static pattern. The recognition is often in the twentieth century called "epiphany." It is the recognition of what Hopkins calls the "inscape" of the object in poetry.

The difference between Browning and Hopkins is that Hopkins dislocates language in order to make his *image* more palpable—to make us feel the force of the bird's soaring in "The Windhover," and the even greater force of its falling movement. The meaning emerges as paradox, and then only by implication—the implication that the active and passive life are equally intense, that Christ triumphed through failure. Browning, on the other hand, tries to achieve the effect of simultaneity through discursive thought itself. That is why Browning is hardly ever at his best where he is obscure; while Hopkins is often at his best where he is obscure. Hopkins goes farther than Browning in symbolizing and myth making.

Yet if you can get certain knotty passages of Browning sufficiently well in mind to leap playfully from idea to idea with the swiftness and freedom of Browning's mind, you actually start a process of association that turns the discursive thought into poetry. Swinburne gives the best description of the pleasure to be derived from the discursive Browning. In comparing Browning with a really obscure poet like Chapman, Swinburne denies that Browning is obscure at all. For obscurity is the product of a confused and chaotic intellect; whereas

> if there is any great quality more perceptible than another in
> Mr. Browning's intellect it is his decisive and incisive faculty

of thought, his sureness and intensity of perception, his rapid
and trenchant resolution of aim. . . . He is something too
much the reverse of obscure; he is too brilliant and subtle for
the ready reader of a ready writer to follow with any certainty
the track of an intelligence which moves with such incessant
rapidity, or even to realize with what spider-like swiftness and
sagacity his building spirit leaps and lightens to and fro and
backward and forward as it lives along the animated line of
its labour, spring from thread to thread and darts from centre
to circumference of the glittering and quivering web of living
thought woven from the inexhaustible stores of his perception
and kindled from the inexhaustible fire of his imagination. . . .
It is hopeless to enjoy the charm or to apprehend the gist of
his writings except with a mind thoroughly alert, an attention
awake at all points.[13]

To return then to our two questions about Browning and
myth, we might say that Browning defined his realism precisely
through opposition to myths as overt subject matter. He was, however, feeling his way to the twentieth-century development,
through realism and psychology, to a psychological use of myth. In
rejecting myth in "Parleying With Gerard de Lairesse," Browning
asks whether he would do better to tell two stories—to repeat the
old myth through realistically apprehended modern circumstances,
repeat the myth of Dryope plucking the lotus blossoms through
the story of an English girl plucking "fruit not fabulous" but
"Apple of English homesteads." "Advantage would it prove or det-
riment / If I saw double?" (118–126).

It is through just such double vision that twentieth-century writers have returned to myth. Browning's phrase recalls Blake's distinction between single vision, which is Newton's way of seeing
facts as just facts, and double vision, which is the capacity to read
facts symbolically.[14] "Oh, we can fancy too!" Browning continues,

> but somehow fact
> Has got to—say, not so much push aside
> Fancy, as to declare its place supplied

By fact unseen but no less fact the same,
Which mind bids sense accept. (149–153)

We have here the modern distinction, derived from Coleridge, between neoclassical fancy and romantic or modern imagination.
The neoclassicist went on using the old myths, not because he believed in them, but because they were decorative and poetical. The
neoclassical painter Lairesse could, in the walk described in his
book on painting, maintain the old mythical view because he was
blind. But the modern artist insists on the truth of his mythical vision—his perception of "the links," in Browning's words, that
"bind / Our earth to heaven" (145–147)—because it evolves out
of direct perception of the facts. The modern artist creates his
own myths and symbols by bringing to the sensuous apprehension
of reality the whole mind or imagination.

This is the essence of modern symbolist theory. Not only "Lairesse" and "Avison," but the whole *Parleyings* can best be understood as Browning's verse essay on symbolism. In "Bernard de
Mandeville," we are told to read the opposition between good and
evil as symbolic of the absolute design of things, and not to take
evil as in itself a substantial reality. If in a ground-plan we were
told that A is the house, we would be foolish to ask where's the
roof to A. But

Why so very much
More foolish than our mortal purblind way
Of seeking in the symbol no mere point
To guide our gaze through what were else inane,
But things—their solid selves? (184–188)

"A myth may teach:" says Browning, "Only, who better would ex-
pound it thus / Must be Euripides not Aeschylus" (204–206).
Euripides did not, like Aeschylus, take myth literally, but understood it as symbolic, as a way of talking about life. Euripides was,
in other words, a realist and therefore a symbolist.

Browning then makes a myth. In the morning of creation, only man was sullen, because he could not like the plants and animals enjoy the sun unconsciously. Man yearned to understand the sun, both in its visible aspect and as an all-informing principle of energy. Man yearned, in other words, to make contact through his mind with the "outside mind" behind the sun, and so love the sun consciously through his understanding. Finally, "Prometheus helped him,"

> Offered an artifice whereby he drew
> Sun's rays into a focus,—plain and true,
> The very Sun in little: made fire burn
> And hence forth do Man service—glass-conglobed
> Though to a pin-point circle—all the same
> Comprising the Sun's self, but Sun disrobed
> Of that else-unconceived essential flame
> Borne by no naked sight.   (301–309)

Prometheus is conceived as having taught man to draw down through a magnifying glass a symbolic representation of the sun, which could be looked at, understood, and used to start a fire, as the sun itself could not. From the symbol, we can "infer immensity," but only the symbol can engage our affection: "In little, light, warmth, life, are blessed—/ Which, in the large, who sees to bless?" (317–319). The whole crucial passage recalls Coleridge's dictum that a true symbol "always partakes of the reality which it renders intelligible." [15]

In "Daniel Bartoli," Browning rejects a kind of symbolism quite different from the modern—the kind set forth in Bartoli's *Dei Simboli Trasportati al Morale*, where the seventeenth-century Jesuit historian does two things Browning does not like. Bartoli repeats implausible legends, and uses them to teach moral lessons; whereas for Browning "historical fact had," as DeVane puts it, "a righteousness of its own." [16] Bartoli is represented as telling an absurdly miraculous legend of a female saint, in order that Browning

may, by way of contrast, tell a story from a memoir, in which a
real girl, acting in plausible circumstances, shows herself to be a
saint in a far more important sense than Bartoli's Saint Scholas-
tica.

In "Christopher Smart," Browning draws from the case of the
poet who once and once only wrote a great poem, and then when
he was in the madhouse, the essential doctrine of symbolist poetry
—the doctrine that poetry is, as Yeats put it, a revelation and
should make the effect of a revelation. Smart achieves his effect
not by giving an exhaustive catalogue of details like modern
naturalists, nor by concerning himself like the aesthetes with
appearances only. Smart uses his *selected* details as symbols—
making them stand for the rest and imbuing them with ideas and
moral meaning. He does not, on the other hand, like the scientists
and their followers, start with abstract laws that when applied to
nature must inevitably devalue it. Smart's ideas are inseparable
from the palpably rendered objects that embody them. He gives
in his "Song to David" the truth about nature, because he
gives "her lovelinesses infinite / In little" (144–145).

In "George Bubb Dodington," Browning shows that this sec-
ond-rate Machiavellian failed in politics, because he operated by
rational laws of calculated self-interest that we all understand too
well. But the great Machiavellian—Browning has Disraeli in mind,
the whole parleying is an attack upon him—is the great charlatan
who, like the artist, knows how to turn himself and his work into
a symbol. He does this by wrapping himself in mystery, operating
by motives we cannot understand.

> No animal—much less our lordly Man—
> Obeys its like . . .
>   Who would use
> Man for his pleasure needs must introduce
> The element that awes Man. Once for all,
> His nature owns a Supernatural.
>   (134–135, 183–191)

In "Francis Furini"—the parleying that makes the most complete statement of symbolist doctrine—Browning is doing something more important than just defending his son's nude paintings. Browning defends the nude in painting by showing that the nude figure is more symbolic than the clothed figure, and symbolic precisely of soul. The artist agonizes

> to adumbrate, trace in dust
> That marvel which we dream the firmament
> Copies in star-device when fancies stray
> Outlining, orb by orb, Andromeda—
> God's best of beauteous and magnificent
> Revealed to earth—the naked female form.
>   (138–143)

The artists who see most clearly God's purpose—to dispense "all gifts / To soul through sense"—are those who "bid us love alone / The type untampered with [i.e., the archetype], the naked star!" (233–247).[17]

In symbolism, there is no high or low; symbolism demonstrates that we can know the so-called high only by knowing the so-called low. There you have the error of the Darwinians—and it is no digression for Browning to associate them with the prudish enemies of the nude—who think that their knowledge of man's low origin negates his spirituality. Once we see that the large subject of "Furini" is symbolism, then the attack on the Darwinians has even more cogency, and Browning's depreciation of man's cognitive faculties has more philosophical justification, than DeVane in his book on the *Parleyings* makes out. We can see how Browning's relativism leads to symbolism when, in criticizing in a letter of 1881 the Darwinian idea that evolution is ungoverned by intelligence, Browning says that "time and space" are "purely conceptions of our own, wholly inapplicable to intelligence of another kind."[18]

The Darwinians do not realize, Browning implies in "Furini," that their theory is itself, by its hierarchical arrangement of nature, an anthropomorphizing symbol system based on intuition of a perfection from which all nature can be scaled downward. The Darwinians, who take an abstract view of nature, looking downward from the top, see only what is lacking. An artist like Furini, instead, who takes his stand within nature, can through loving penetration of a particular living thing uncover "Marvel at hiding under marvel, pluck / Veil after veil from Nature" (395–396), and thus see the living thing as pointing upward, as symbolizing the whole perfect scheme.

The pre-eminence that the Darwinians themselves give man derives not from man's power or even from his knowledge. For the proportions of nature are so incommensurate with our cognitive faculties that we can never know nature as it is in itself:

> . . . what *is* minuteness—yonder vault
> Speckled with suns, or this the millionth—thing,
> . . . that on some insect's wing
> Helps to make out in dyes the mimic star?
>
> (293–296)

The thing that gives us pre-eminence is our moral sense, our intuition of perfection; and all the individual knows for sure is his consciousness of himself as having that sense. The individual finds in and through his self-consciousness what we should call anthropomorphizing images—"thus blend / I, and all things perceived, in one Effect" (361–362)—which, by some mysterious law, he understands as corresponding to the external world. What the individual knows, in other words—and here Browning comes close to Blake's "Where man is not, nature is barren" [19]—is *imagined* nature.

Like Andromeda, the individual clings to his "rock-spit of self-knowledge" (410), with the sea of ignorance surging round. Art teaches him about spirit by directing his gaze precisely toward the body, toward

Those incommensurably marvellous
Contrivances which furnish forth the house
Where soul has sway! Though Master keep aloof,
Signs of His presence multiply from roof
To basement of the building. . . .
                                He's away, no doubt,
But what if, all at once, you come upon
A startling proof—not that the Master gone
Was present lately—but that something—whence
Light comes—has pushed Him into residence?
                                            (533-543)

Suddenly, in what we should call an epiphany, the physical details
light up from within, manifesting the invisible in the visible, turning into what we should call a symbol.

    Browning is trying to say what Yeats says more pithily—that
"Man can embody truth but he cannot know it." [20] The passage
even concludes with Yeats's favorite circular symbol of the serpent
with its tail in its mouth.

"Was such the symbol's meaning,—old, uncouth—
That circle of the serpent, tail in mouth?
Only by looking low, ere looking high,
Comes penetration of the mystery."   (544-547)

    In the *Parleyings*—which is the most complete statement of his
maturest thought—Browning answers the problems of his time by
suggesting that we change the nature of the questions we put to
the universe, that we turn upon all aspects of life double rather
than single vision. Had Browning been able to realize such doctrine in his art, had he been able to make his fragmentary glimpses
of life symbolic of the whole, of an absolute vision, he would have
broken through to the modern mythical method. He would have
broken through to a final clarity of vision and style and been one
of the great poets of English literature. As it is, he is a poet of enduring interest—partly because his very faults show that he was

turning analytic thought against itself, that he understood what
had to be done.

I would like to conclude, however, by mentioning a few poems
in which Browning does use, and with great success, the modern
mythical method. The first is the famous "Childe Roland," where
the meaning is not extractable but is simply *in* the pattern of
movement. Although the poem dramatizes a reference in a well-
known play to a well-known figure, it hardly deals with one of Arnold's grand, enduring subjects. Browning has made in the poem
his own private myth.

The second is a major work. Yet it is undeservedly overlooked in
courses on, and discussions of, Browning. I refer to *Balaustion's
Adventure*, in which the Greek girl Balaustion retells Euripides'
Alcestis as translated by Browning. Balaustion is fresh, gentle,
sweet, compassionate. She has what Browning thought of as the
very best qualities of nineteenth-century sensibility; so that, in fil-
tering Euripides' play through her, Browning makes us feel how
modern in its sensibility the play is, and how modern Euripides is.
He makes us understand why, in *The Ring and the Book*, the Pope
says that Euripides was a Christian before the advent of the Christian era. For without giving the *Alcestis* a Christian construction
—and it is a good thing that Balaustion herself is a contemporary
of Euripides—Browning makes us feel, through his rendition, that
any person has a Christian heart who understands that love is a
greater force than death.

Published in 1871, *Balaustion's Adventure* was written directly
after *The Ring and the Book*. I certainly agree with DeVane, in
the *Browning Handbook*, that *Balaustion's Adventure* ought to be
considered as closing—which is to say as within—Browning's best
period. It is actually more successful than *The Ring and the Book*
in achieving what it sets out to do. If I hesitate to rank it above or
even with *The Ring and the Book*, it is only because the poem is

after all mainly Euripides. Yet I am not sure this matters. We probably ought to understand the poem as we understand Ezra Pound's translations—as a creative appropriation of ancient material, a way of giving an ancient poet a historical consciousness he himself could not have had. Eliot said of Pound that he "is much more modern, in my opinion, when he deals with Italy and Provence, than when he deals with modern life." [21] This way of being modern is what Eliot means by the mythical method.

Eliot means something quite different from that use of established classical mythology so expertly traced by Douglas Bush in *Mythology and the Romantic Tradition*. Bush is mainly right when he says that "Browning was not a poet of mythological imagination; the few moments in which he seems to deserve that name only emphasize his normal character as a novelist in verse." I demur, however, when Bush gives as evidence the fact that in Browning's Greek poems "the Greece he presents is a mixture of the completely real and the completely unreal. Whatever solid properties can be seen or touched are Greek; the psychological motives he evolves are usually not Greek." [22] The modern mythical method challenges and re-establishes mythical pattern precisely through realism and through psychology in the modern sense; though the poem will indeed be novelistic where mythical pattern is not re-established. That is the difference between the novelistic *Ring and the Book*, where the re-establishment of mythical pattern is only incidental, and the Greek *Balaustion*, where it is central.

The Ring and the Book and *Balaustion* employ the mythical method from opposite sides. For we start in *Balaustion* with the myth or pattern, and the narrator undertakes to make it real—to describe for us, as she says, the human expressions beneath the masks of the mythical characters. The myth of Alcestis is another version of the Andromeda-Perseus myth; Heracles, who brings back Alcestis from the dead, is even a descendant of Perseus. The thing Balaustion does is to draw out, through her comments on

Euripides' tragicomedy, the underlying tragicomic pattern—the pattern of impasse and miracle—that is at the heart of Browning's view of the world and of his Christian faith.

Heracles' entrance into the play is beautifully interpreted by Balaustion. Left to themselves, human motives and the logic of events have led to an impasse; Alcestis must die and there is no help for it. But then, suddenly, there breaks upon the scene "that great interrupting voice" (1032). There is certainly a Christian analogue in the fact that the appearance of the god is heralded (a touch not really in Euripides) by his voice. "Sudden into the midst of sorrow," says Balaustion,

> leapt
> Along with the gay cheer of that great voice,
> Hope, joy, salvation: Herakles was here!
> Himself, o' the threshold, sent his voice on first
> To herald all that human and divine
> I' the weary happy face of him,—half God,
> Half man, which made the god-part God the more.
>
> (1045-51)

It is because Heracles was a man that we can see as miraculous his willingness to labor for men for no reason other than his love— that he can, in other words, symbolize Divinity.

The movement is assimilated to the pattern of death and rebirth in the vegetation cycle. When Heracles goes gaily off to bring back Alcestis from the dead, Balaustion comments:

> I think this is the authentic sign and seal
> Of Godship, that it ever waxes glad,
> And more glad, until gladness blossoms, bursts
> Into a rage to suffer for mankind,
> And recommence at sorrow:

just as, Balaustion continues, the flower is willing, at the height of its bloom, to drop its seed—

once more die into the ground,
Taste cold and darkness and oblivion there:
And thence rise, tree-like grow through pain to joy,
More joy and most joy,—do man good again.
                                                    (1918–29)

The same cyclical pattern governs the moral and spiritual life of
each individual. After Alcestis's husband Admetus has said everything except the truth—that he ought not to have allowed Alcestis
to die for him—after Admetus has told all the lies: after, in Balaustion's metaphor, "the last of bubbles broke" leaving the surface "placid"—then "up swam / To the surface the drowned
truth, in dreadful change" (2047–50). The metaphor describes
perfectly the psychological movement of the best dramatic monologues—where it is after the speaker has told all his lies, that inad-
vertently, and as if of its own accord, the truth rises to the surface.
Only here we see how the deepest psychology leads back to a
mythical pattern that is itself imbedded in the very order of things.

We see in the tragicomic pattern of impasse and miracle the
meaning behind the Andromeda myth. The miracle in the *Alcestis*
is, as Browning interprets it, the transformation of Admetus's consciousness. It is when Admetus—who feared death as the worst of
evils—suddenly *sees* "how dear is death, / How loveable the dead
are" (1952–53) that Alcestis is restored to him as the external sign
of the internal transformation. The same thing happens in "Childe
Roland," where a transformation of consciousness makes the dark
tower appear and turns all the facts that spell defeat into victory.
The logic of events leads to winter; *spring* is the miracle. Transformation of consciousness is the way through the impasse logic leads
to! This is Browning's understanding of the Incarnation, the
descent of Divinity into human life.

Such collapsing of diverse events into a single pattern is at the
heart of the mythical method. An interest in *Balaustion* might
lead to revaluation of certain other neglected poems—of, for example, that strange and difficult late lyric, "Numpholeptos." "Numpholeptos" is like "Andrea del Sarto"—in its Tennysonian echoes

(echoes here of "Tithonus"), in its sustained contrast between images of silver and gold, and in the speaker's final choice of continued enslavement to the lady against whom he has said so much.
The comparison helps us see that the lady of "Numpholeptos" is
another kind of Lucrezia, one who torments by being all too ideal-
istic and sexlessly pure. The comparison helps us see that the case
here is still psychological. But the psychology is in "Numpholeptos" projected through a peculiarly modern penetration of mythical figures, the nymph and nymph-enraptured lover, who are themselves seen as emerging out of natural phenomena—the cold radi-
ance of the moon: and the white light that is refracted through
the dust of earth into warm hues that, like the man of the poem,
go forth only to return and die into their origin in the white light.

An interest in Balaustion might suggest that Browning did, after
all, go farther than I have indicated toward projecting a total vision of life. *Balaustion* should certainly make us pay attention to
the beautiful little lyric on spring with which Browning, in "Parleying With Gerard de Lairesse," concludes his argument against
the use of classical mythology. This is, he says, the modern poet's
way of making rhyme about, say, the miracle of spring which "the
Greek Bard sadly greets: / 'Spring for the tree and herb—no Spring
for us!'" The modern lyric, through a precise rendition of spring
flowers, suggests all that the myths tell us about death and rebirth.

> Dance, yellows and whites and reds,—
> Lead your gay orgy, leaves, stalks, heads
> Astir with the wind in the tulip-beds!
>
> There's sunshine; scarcely wind at all
> Disturbs starved grass and daisies small
> On a certain mound by a churchyard wall.
>
> Daisies and grass be my heart's bedfellows
> On the mound wind spares and sunshine mellows:
> Dance you, reds and whites and yellows!
>
> (426–434)

Christianity, Browning implies, makes such realism possible by confirming our deepest intuition that the vegetation cycle is, indeed, symbolic of our fate after death.

"Numpholeptos" and the lyric on spring work from opposite directions—the first from the archetype to the human situation or seen fact, the second from the seen fact to the "fact unseen but no less fact the same." They both, however, employ double vision, and thus show how realism and psychology lead to the distinctively modern recovery of symbol and myth.

THE
NEW
NATURE
POETRY

What has happened to nature poetry? Ask this question of your up-to-date kind of poetry reader, and you will get a stare of blank amazement. There isn't any, he will mutter, although he will soon concede that there *is* Robert Frost. If he admires Frost, he will probably assure you that Frost is no mere nature poet, the implication being that nature poetry can no longer have serious relevance. He will have behind him the authority of critical opinion, of even Joseph Warren Beach, who, in *The Concept of Nature in Nineteenth-Century English Poetry*, the most thorough study of the subject, says that the very name and concept of nature have virtually disappeared from twentieth-century poetry. Frost himself is not a nature poet, says Beach, since he writes not about nature but about this, that and the other thing in the country.

Beach has in mind the philosophical and protoreligious concept of nature that flourished in the eighteenth century and was already on its way out in the nineteenth. The religion of nature derived from Newton's demonstration that everything from the fall of an apple to the movement of planets is governed by a single law. To

people whose Christianity was waning, a nature so orderly seemed
to offer new evidence of God's existence and a new source of religious emotion. But the religion of nature was threatened, first, by
early nineteenth-century geology, which found in the rocks evidence of catastrophes that had wiped out whole species, and finally
by Darwin's theory that the evolution of species is governed by a
mindless force called natural selection. Under these assaults, nature poetry declined. Swinburne tried to be optimistic about post-
Darwinian nature, and Hardy was definitely pessimistic about it.
But both were being anthropomorphic still, at a time when the ex-
citing new concept, the only one that could inspire conviction, was
that of the mindlessness of nature, its nonhuman otherness—a
concept *attempting* at least to transcend optimism and pessimism.

Now it is just this sense of nature that a number of contemporary American and British poets render superbly; so that far from
being extinct, nature poetry has enjoyed a revival. It is better than
it has been in a long time. I would like, through a few examples
from contemporary poets, to call attention to the existence and
relevance of this new nature poetry. But why, if this poetry is so
good, should it be necessary to point out its existence? Because, I
think, the term *nature poetry* has fallen into such disrepute that
no one wants to apply it to poems he likes; and because critics
who are looking for the eighteenth-century concept of nature will
not find it in poems that are precisely trying to rescue nature, as it
is in itself, from the outmoded concept.

Take as an example of the new sense of nature Wallace Stevens's "The Snow Man," which contrasts the inevitably anthropomorphic human apprehension of a winter landscape with the landscape as it might be apprehended by the mindless "mind" of a
snow man. "One must have a mind of winter / . . . And have
been cold a long time"

> not to think
> Of any misery in the sound of the wind,
> In the sound of a few leaves,

Which is the sound of the land
Full of the same wind
That is blowing in the same bare place

For the listener, who listens in the snow,
And, nothing himself, beholds
Nothing that is not there and the nothing that is.[1]

Or take Marianne Moore's poem about the sea, which she calls
"A Grave" to suggest, as I understand it, the unmeaning nullity
of the sea. She tells us in the opening lines that she will render
the sea not from the human point of view, but as it is in itself:

Man looking into the sea,
taking the view from those who have as much right to it as
    you have to it yourself,
it is human nature to stand in the middle of a thing,
but you cannot stand in the middle of this;
the sea has nothing to give but a well excavated grave.

And the poem ends:

The wrinkles progress among themselves in a phalanx—
    beautiful under networks of foam,
and fade breathlessly while the sea rustles in and out of the
    seaweed;
the birds swim through the air at top speed, emitting cat-
    calls as heretofore—
the tortoise-shell scourges about the feet of the cliffs, in
    motion beneath them;
and the ocean, under the pulsation of lighthouses and noise
    of bell-buoys,
advances as usual, looking as if it were not that ocean in
    which dropped things are bound to sink—
in which if they turn and twist, it is neither with volition
    nor consciousness.[2]

One might almost suppose for a moment that the ocean has volition and consciousness, but this is a delusion.

In the middle of the last century, Ruskin coined the phrase, "pathetic fallacy," which defines among other things the modern reaction against the eighteenth- and nineteenth-century style of nature poetry. The pathetic fallacy is the false description that occurs when, under the pressure of strong emotion, the poet projects human feelings into natural objects (Kingsley's "cruel, crawling foam"). Ruskin considers the pathetic fallacy justified as long as the distortion is psychologically valid, appropriate to the observer's emotion. Such poetry, in which the emotions are "strong enough to vanquish, partly, the intellect, and make it believe what they choose," can be good poetry of the second order. But in poetry of the first order, like Dante's, "the intellect also rises, till it is strong enough to assert its rule against, or together with, the utmost efforts of the passions; and the whole man stands in an iron glow, white hot, perhaps, but still strong, and in no wise evaporating." Poetry of the first order retains the "plain and leafy fact" of the primrose, "whatever and how many soever the associations and passions may be that crowd around it." [3] Not only does Ruskin anticipate Eliot's attack on the "dissociation of sensibility" from thought, but he sets forth the program of the best twentieth-century nature poetry, which defines itself precisely by opposing, or seeming to oppose, the pathetic fallacy (one cannot perhaps get round it), and thus extending the range of nineteenth-century projectiveness. For to feel in nature an unalterably alien, even an unfeeling, existence is to carry empathy several steps farther than did the nineteenth-century poets who felt in nature a life different from but compatible with ours.

That is the point of the Stevens and Marianne Moore lines I have quoted. It is the point of Frost's poem, "The Need of Being Versed in Country Things," about a burnt-down farmhouse. The birds fly in and out of the abandoned barn, "Their murmur more like the sigh we sigh / From too much dwelling on what has been," but their sympathetic response is illusory. "Yet for them the lilac renewed its leaf," we are told,

> For them there was really nothing sad.
> But though they rejoiced in the nest they kept,
> One had to be versed in country things
> Not to believe the phoebes wept [4]

—not to commit the pathetic fallacy. The strategy of the last two
lines is like the strategy of Marianne Moore's last two lines; only
Frost lets us down so much more gently. In both poems, the incli-
nation to commit the pathetic fallacy is a sign that the object is
loved, as is Stevens's projection into the snow man. But in Stevens
and Marianne Moore, the difference between man and nature is
wider, more irreconcilable, more dangerous than in Frost. In Frost
the life of man weaves so inextricably in and out of nature that it
comes as a surprise to the speaker to discover that they are not
identical. And the difference poses no real threat. The perception
of it is simply salutary. This makes Frost less radically twentieth-
century in his sense of nature than Stevens and Marianne Moore.

The difference in Frost often defines itself against such domestic
considerations as that of utility and ownership. In "Going for
Water," the speaker gains an insight into water not as something
to be used or owned but as it is in itself; and in "The Wood-Pile,"
the speaker realizes that the precisely cut and measured cord of fire
wood, unaccountably abandoned "far from a useful fireplace," has
another use: "To warm the frozen swamp as best it could / With
the slow smokeless burning of decay." There is a suggestion of
danger in the famous "Stopping by Woods on a Snowy Evening,"
where the speaker, who has interrupted his journey homeward and
trespassed on another's property to watch the woods fill up with
snow, pulls himself away reluctantly:

> The woods are lovely, dark and deep,
> But I have promises to keep,
> And miles to go before I sleep,
> And miles to go before I sleep.

The momentary insight into the nonhuman otherness of nature is salutary, but to prolong it is to seek unconsciousness, individual extinction, before your time. In "Come In," the speaker, who comes at evening to the edge of a dark wood, hears thrush music inside,

> Almost like a call to come in
> To the dark and lament.
>
> But no, I was out for stars:
> I would not come in.
> I meant not even if asked,
> And I hadn't been.

To consider nature purposively dangerous is also to commit the pathetic fallacy. Besides, nature in Frost never is so dangerous that his speakers cannot protect themselves against it.[5]

Frost takes into account nature's destructiveness, but his examples of it are seldom very frightening. The whispering scythe of "Mowing" must in performing its useful labor cut down the pale orchises and scare a bright green snake. Before they "can mount again," the leaves of "In Hardwood Groves" must "go down into the dark decayed." But the scythe is whispering in effect that all is well; while toward the natural cycle, the theme that gave birth to tragedy and religion, Frost takes a merely commonsense attitude: "However it is in some other world / I know that this is the way in ours." In "Storm Fear," the speaker, waking to hear the wind and snow seem to challenge him to come out and fight, is glad not to accept the challenge and wonders in despair whether he and his family will have the strength to save themselves in the morning. But even in this poem, we know that the despair is a passing mood, that in the morning they will have the strength.

Death itself is adumbrated as a sleep in two perfect poems, "After Apple-Picking" and "An Old Man's Winter Night." In both poems, the man falls asleep when his work is almost but not quite finished, his sleep corresponds to the sleep of nature in winter, and the natural process takes over his unfinished work. Forget-

ting what he came to do in a roomful of barrels, the old man of
the latter poem consigns to the moon his snow upon the roof, his
icicles, and sleeps.

> One aged man—one man—can't keep a house,
> A farm, a countryside, or if he can,
> It's thus he does it of a winter night.

This shows harmony with nature—except that the old man's
"clomping" in and out of the room makes an almost supernatural
disturbance, scaring the cellar and the outer night; while the lamp
he carries keeps him from seeing out-of-doors, it lights only himself with his own thoughts. The noise and the thoughts suggest
the slightest disharmony with nature.

In "After Apple-Picking," it is also thoughts of the day's and
season's apple-picking, of the unpicked apples and of "magnified
apples" better than any on the boughs that will "trouble" the
speaker's oncoming sleep, "whatever sleep it is." Is it a night's or
winter's dream of the day's or autumn's activity; and is such a
troubled slumber natural or supernatural?

> The woodchuck could say whether it's like his
> Long sleep, as I describe its coming on,
> Or just some human sleep.

"Just," of course, from the woodchuck's point of view; for the
speculation reminds me at least of Keats's fancy that our next life
will be a spiritual repetition of this one "in a finer tone."

It is not to quarrel with these poems—who could be anything
but grateful for perfection?—to say that they are idyls. The narra-
tives about people, like "A Servant to Servants," are sometimes
tragic. But there is in the nature poems (including Darwinian
poems, like "On a Bird Singing in Its Sleep" and "Acceptance") a
harmony even in the disharmony; they leave out the agony of
dying. Here as elsewhere Frost's acceptances are won without an-
guish—partly because the danger is not dangerous enough, partly

because of Frost's personal strength, which is always at least equal
to the danger. Certainly "Design" is a dark poem:

> I found a dimpled spider, fat and white,
> On a white heal-all, holding up a moth
> Like a white piece of rigid satin cloth—
> Assorted characters of death and blight
> Mixed ready to begin the morning right,
> Like the ingredients of a witches' broth—
> A snow-drop spider, a flower like a froth,
> And dead wings carried like a paper kite.

But Frost cuts off the implications that might threaten us, by concluding with a rather pointless reflection. What brought that design together? What, but design; if, indeed, there is design.

> What but design of darkness to appall?—
> If design govern in a thing so small.

Frost's darkest nature poem is "Desert Places," where the snow
and the dark wood are unambiguously desolate: "Snow falling and
night falling, fast, oh, fast / . . . The woods around it have it—it
is theirs."

> The loneliness includes me unawares.

> And lonely as it is that loneliness
> Will be more lonely ere it will be less—
> A blanker whiteness of benighted snow
> With no expression, nothing to express.

> They cannot scare me with their empty spaces
> Between stars—on stars where no human race is.
> I have it in me so much nearer home
> To scare myself with my own desert places.

But even here, where Frost sees nature as a void and takes into account the implications of science, he turns into a kind of consolation that perception of an internal void which would be for an-

other poet the most terrifying perception of all. "Loneliness . . .
will be less" together with "scare myself" suggest that the scare is
the illusory thing, almost a game (scaring one's self and others) of
spooks.

Such resistance comes of sheer biological vitality, a self-preserv-
ing common sense, which Reginald Cook calls Frost's *sabiduría*—a
Spanish word meaning "the wisdom of a people welling up in any
one of its articulate members." [6] It is *sabiduría* that keeps Frost at
the edge of the "dark wood," keeps him from following his insights through to their logical implications, from risking the destructiveness of abstract thought. "The world's one globe," he says
in "Build Soil,"

> human society
> Another softer globe that slightly flattened
> Rests on the world, and clinging slowly rolls.
> We have our own round shape to keep unbroken.
> The world's size has no more to do with us
> Than has the universe's.

He is able to shrug off those conflicts between man and nature,
thought and reality, head and heart, science and religion, which
since the romantic period have torn other poets apart.

The result is a poetry that delivers us from the poignancy of the
historical moment to place us in contact with a survival-making
eternal folk wisdom. We can live by Frost's poetry as we could not
by Yeats's or Pound's. Yet his poetry, although it must rank high
in our affections, is not likely to be the favorite poetry of the most
serious readers, just because Frost does not call into play all our
faculties; he does not make poetry of our ideas, which in modern
times have mainly to do with our sense of the age. The poets who
have since the romantic period made the greatest impact are precisely those poets who have made us most aware of the historical
moment, having themselves not merely known about but felt the
conflicts of their age.

That is the difference between Wordsworth's nature poetry and Frost's. To talk about nature in Wordsworth's way was at the turn of the nineteenth century to be at the forefront of thought, to take into account the science, philosophy and psychology of the age, its religious skepticism, the French Revolution, the problem of the modern analytic intellect as the destroyer of feeling. If nature was orderly and the self an association of external impressions, then a life in the country would insure you the most favorable impressions. It would afford evidence of God's existence, an alternative or supplement to revolution and political reform for man's improvement, and an object that could still inspire feelings, even supernatural apprehensions. The deliberate return to nature went with the deliberate cultivation of the feelings as the necessary antidote to the conditions of modern life. No nineteenth-century reader could share in one of Wordsworth's epiphanies—one of his revelations through visible nature of "the life of things"—without a very poignant awareness of victory over the age. That is what John Stuart Mill meant when he called Wordsworth "the poet of unpoetical [distinctively modern] natures"; it is what Matthew Arnold meant when he said that in "this iron time" Wordsworth taught us to feel again.[7]

Now Frost's sense of nature as manageable is very like Wordsworth's, as is his method of conveying that sense. For Frost, too, gives us little dramatic actions that culminate in epiphanies. But Frost's are timid epiphanies, for they deliberately stop short of, where they do not explicitly repudiate, philosophical implications; and they do not arise, as they often do in Wordsworth, from an impasse in thought, thought grounded in the age. Frost's moments of awareness are accidents that could happen to any one in any age. The sign of this is that they do not change the speaker who simply goes back to his business; whereas Wordsworth's speakers undergo a measure of conversion. That is why his poems can be read in sequence as an evolution from eighteenth-century doubt through romantic transcendentalism to Christian orthodoxy.

In the sheer power to render nature, Frost may well be our best nature poet since Wordsworth. Yet it is because Frost's rendition of nature is so like Wordsworth's that he does not play in our time the role Wordsworth played in his, that he leads us away from rather than to the center of the preoccupations of the time. For Frost cannot embrace the transcendentalism that his way of seeing nature suggests; but neither does he have the so much wilder sense of nature that our latest nature philosophy requires. Our nature philosophy has been made not only by Darwin but by Freud and Frazer. It connects not only man's body but his mind and culture to the primeval ooze; and that sense of nature is difficult to convey in poems about the cultivated countryside of England or New England.

Dylan Thomas manages miraculously to revive, through the usual settings, Wordsworth's pantheistic vision—perhaps because Thomas was from Wales and more primitive than his contemporaries, but also because he was sophisticated and took into account Darwin, Freud, Frazer, along with the modern interest in theology and paradox. He connects our most metaphysical ideas with, in the poem of that title, "The force that through the green fuse drives the flower." And when in "A Refusal to Mourn," he speaks of dying as entering

> again the round
> Zion of the water bead
> And the synagogue of the ear of corn,

he is at once more biological and more theological than Wordsworth, and therefore modern. But the paradox at the end, "After the first death, there is no other," [8] is the same as in Wordsworth's "A Slumber Did My Spirit Seal"—that the girl achieves immortality through her very mortality in nature.

It is more usually, however, about the tropics or the sea, the

primeval sources of life, or about the lower forms of life, that contemporary poets are apt to write when they do in our age what
Wordsworth did in his—when they convey in their sense of nature
their sense of the age. Wallace Stevens is fond of seascapes, Flor-
ida settings and tropical birds. Marianne Moore goes farther afield
with her tropical lizards, her fish and mollusks, her frigate pelican,
her small Sahara field-mouse, her mongoose and cobra. Theodore
Roethke writes about roots in a root cellar where "Even the dirt
kept breathing a small breath" ("Root Cellar"), and the minute
"lives on a leaf" including "bacterial creepers" ("The Minimal").[9]

One of the reasons the new nature poetry is not recognizable as
such is that it is so often about animals rather than landscapes.
The poet is less likely to commit the pathetic fallacy with animals,
for they have a consciousness of their own. Then animals do for
the landscape what the older kind of nature poet had to do himself—they bring it to life. They are the landscape crystallized into
movement and consciousness; so that Marianne Moore begins
"The Plumet Basilisk" by distinguishing this Costa Rican lizard
from the landscape we take him for at first:

> In blazing driftwood
>   the green keeps showing at the same place;
>   as, intermittently, the fire-opal shows blue and green.

The new nature poetry deals often with the line between nonliv-
ing and living unconsciousness—as its way of evoking "the life of
things." For the new nature poetry is really about that concept by
which living unconsciousness has come to be understood as a form
of consciousness and, paradoxically, the most vital form of it.

Nature poetry, which must always be about the living principle
in nature, declined as it became more and more difficult to assert
that principle, especially after Darwin seemed to remove mind
from even the higher forms of life. The new concept of the unconscious, instead, has extended mind to the very borderline between
animate and inanimate nature. For it has connected the substra-

tum of our minds with the minds of the very lowest reaches of animal life, thus reanimating all of nature and making nature poetry possible again. We have already seen how, by emphasizing the deadness of the dynamic and life-giving sea, Marianne Moore makes us feel how nearly alive the sea is, thus enhancing our sense of what it is to be alive.

She starts higher up the scale in

THE FISH

wade
through black jade.
  Of the crow-blue mussel-shells, one keeps
  adjusting the ash-heaps;
      opening and shutting itself like

an
injured fan

to move down, through the equivocally living mussel-shells, to barnacles stirred into life, and only thus distinguished from the sea, by "submerged shafts of the / sun," moving

          themselves with spotlight swiftness
    into the crevices—
      in and out, illuminating

the
turquoise sea
of bodies

to the unalive erosive action of the sea against the cliff. This inorganic process is more dynamic than the jelly-fish, crabs and toadstools that "slide" under its impetus "each on the other." Yet the emphasis in the end on its deadness and lack of reproductive capacity reminds us of the mysterious point where inorganic turns into organic process. The "chasm-side" of the cliff is

> dead.
> Repeated
>   evidence has proved that it can live
>   on what can not revive
>   its youth. The sea grows old in it.

D. H. Lawrence's rank as a poet is still unsettled. But Lawrence had the genius to see the way things were tending and, in his animal poems, sets the style for the new nature poetry. In "Fish," he is interested in the strangeness of a life that not only inhabits an element different from ours, but that is one with this element and therefore without knowledge and without self, an emblem of perfect unconsciousness.

> As the waters roll
> Roll you.
> The waters wash,
> You wash in oneness
> And never emerge.
>
> Never know,
> Never grasp.
>
> Your life a sluice of sensation along your sides,
>
> . . .
>
> Even snakes lie together.
>
> But oh, fish, that rock in water,
> You lie only with the waters;
> One touch.

Near the end, he evokes the horror and beauty of this utterly alien life:

> I have waited with a long rod
> And suddenly pulled a gold-and-greenish, lucent fish
>   from below,
> And had him fly like a halo round my head,
> Lunging in the air on the line.

Unhooked his gorping, water-honey mouth,
And seen his horror-tilted eye,
His red-gold, water-precious, mirror-flat bright eye;
And felt him beat in my hand, with his mucous, leaping
    life-throb,

then, perhaps too didactically, makes explicit the moral of many
recent animal poems:

And my heart accused itself
Thinking: *I am not the measure of creation.
This is beyond me, this fish.
His God stands outside my God.*

This is the moral of Lawrence's best known animal poem,
"Snake," in which the golden brown snake, who contains within
himself the tropical heat and volcanic energy of a Sicilian July,
seems, as he retreats into his black hole, "a king in exile," the alien
god of our submerged unconscious and libidinal life.[10]

In his stunning poem, "Pike," the young English poet, Ted
Hughes, makes even more apparent than Lawrence his resistance
to the pathetic fallacy; for Hughes intensifies both the nonhu-
manness and the gorgeousness of his fish.

Pike, three inches long, perfect
Pike in all parts, green tigering the gold.
Killers from the egg: the malevolent aged grin.
They dance on the surface among the flies.

Or move, stunned by their own grandeur,
Over a bed of emerald, silhouette
Of submarine delicacy and horror.
A hundred feet long in their world.

In ponds, under the heat-struck lily pads—
Gloom of their stillness:
Logged on last year's black leaves, watching upwards.
Or hung in an amber cavern of weeds

The jaws' hooked clamp and fangs
Not to be changed at this date;
A life subdued to its instrument;
The gills kneading quietly, and the pectorals.

Three we kept behind glass,

. . .

Suddenly there were two. Finally one

With a sag belly and the grin it was born with.

In the end, Hughes takes just the leap Frost does not take in "De-sign." For the pike are turned into an idea of menace—of a slow, waiting time outside our sense of time, of a terror outside the reality framed by our petty human contrivances. The scene shifts to an ancient pond of legendary depth that held "Pike too immense to stir, so immense and old," the poet

silently cast and fished
With the hair frozen on my head
For what might move, for what eye might move.
The still splashes on the dark pond,

Owls hushing the floating woods
Frail on my ear against the dream
Darkness beneath night's darkness had freed,
That rose slowly towards me, watching.

In Hughes's "Ghost Crabs," this same terror, represented by giant crabs that "emerge / An invisible disgorging of the sea's cold," is shut out by our toys, "the world of our possessions"; but the crabs are called "God's only toys." [11] Lawrence and Hughes exaggerate, to the point where nature is seen as supernatural because we cannot keep it in abeyance, Frost's trick of locating nature just a step beyond utility and our vision into the "dark wood."

Theodore Roethke, instead, longs for the pre-conscious existence of nature. In "Snake," he would "be that thing" the snake is, "The pure, sensuous form." But in the late "Meditation at Oyster River," he would regress even farther, to formlessness. He longs to dissolve the configuration of self, and be one with the free-running river tides that flow into the bay.

Over the low, barnacled, elephant-colored rocks,
Come the first tide-ripples, moving, almost without sound, toward me,
Running along the narrow furrows of the shore, the rows of dead clam
    shells;
Then a runnel behind me, creeping closer,
Alive with tiny striped fish, and young crabs climbing in and out of
    the water.

The poet wants for himself the prelapsarian existence of Lawrence's fish:

Now, in this waning of light,
I rock with the motion of morning;
In the cradle of all that is,
I'm lulled into half sleep
By the lapping of water,
Cries of the sandpiper.
Water's my will, and my way,
And the spirit runs, intermittently,
In and out of the small waves,

and water itself, in the final image of dissolution and salvation, is dissolved into light:

In the first of the moon,
All's a scattering,
A shining.

Lawrence concludes "Fish" by saying:

In the beginning
Jesus was called The Fish . . .
And in the end.

Lawrence thus establishes the dialectic by which, in dealing with the evolution out of, and the regression back to, formlessness, the new nature poetry takes us over from water to animals to gods.

Light is the vivifying principle in Wallace Stevens's "Tattoo," where the light, crawling "like a spider" over the landscape and under your eyelids, brings both your eyes and the landscape to life:

> There are filaments of your eyes
> On the surface of the water
> And in the edges of the snow.

Along with the sense of nature's otherness goes the sense that it cannot be known in itself, that we can know only our own perception of it—not only our individual perception but also (and this is where the new nature poetry goes beyond that of the nineteenth century and of Frost with his "dark wood") the perception our civilization, our style of art, gives us. Thus Stevens gives "Thirteen Ways of Looking at a Blackbird," and tells us how the round jar he placed on a hill in Tennessee gave a shape to nature, "made the slovenly wilderness / Surround that hill." The jar made nature *see*able.

There is a dispute as to whether Stevens in "Anecdote of the Jar" is praising art or nature. I would say both, on the evidence of his other poems. Art is not the same as nature, but our perception of even natural beauty depends on an aesthetic—an aesthetic which, like consciousness itself, is a crystallization of the landscape but with an even more inexplicable difference. The rendition of nature through an art style calls attention to the fact that nature can be known only through an aesthetic. In "The Idea of Order at Key West," we hear the sea because we hear the girl's song:

> It may be that in all her phrases stirred
> The grinding water and the gasping wind;
> But it was she and not the sea we heard.
>
> For she was the maker of the song she sang.

Thus the rendition of nature through an art style enhances our sense of nature's otherness and unknowability. It is no accident that Stevens and Marianne Moore are concerned not only with nature but also with styles of art and civilization—that they are known even for a certain preciosity. For there seems to be a direct proportion between our sense of nature as wild and nonhuman, and our appreciation of just the artificial surface, the distinctively "aesthetic" quality, of art and civilization.[12]

Marianne Moore, who can render the sea naturalistically, gives us in "The Steeple-Jack" the same sense of its dynamics when she renders it in the static style of Dürer: "water etched / with waves as formal as the scales / on a fish." To render the jerboa or Sahara field-mouse, she starts "The Jerboa" with an almost suffocating evocation of the highly artificial and excessively opulent beauty of the oppressive civilization of the Pharaohs; and she does this largely by cataloguing the multitude (the section is called "Too Much") of African animals they tamed, carved, worshipped: took as models for and forced into their art style. After tightening the spring for fifteen such stanzas, she releases it in two stanzas where she evokes by contrast the happiness, beauty, freedom of the jerboa, who "lives without water," in the midst of nothingness, and without reference to men: "but one would not be he / who has nothing but plenty."

In "The Plumet Basilisk," she no sooner brings the lizard to life from the "blazing driftwood" we take him for at first, than she says: "In Costa Rica the true Chinese lizard face / is found, of the amphibious falling dragon, the living fire- / work"—reminding us that the lizard was the dragon of art and mythology, even a god. Alarmed, he "dives to the stream-bed, hiding as the chieftain with gold / body hid in / Guatavita Lake"—a reference, the Notes tell us, to the yearly ceremony in which the king, "powdered with gold-dust as symbolic of the sun," plunged into the lake. Recalling Frazer, we may infer that the king renewed his vitality or godhead by returning to the source of it, just as the lizard at this moment returns to his underwater "basilica." "The plumet portrays / ," we are told later on, "mythology's wish / to be interchangeably man and fish." And the basilisk is rendered in its relation to other lizards—and to the whole of evolution, from water, through the Reptilian Age (the birds toddle in and out among sea lizards' tails "laid criss-cross, alligator-style"), to the dragons carved over the door of the bourse in Copenhagen. His retreat in the end from the observer is a return in consciousness to the legendary past of treasures guarded by dragons ("Thinking himself hid among the yet unfound jade axe- / heads") and a physical return to the water ("his basilisk cocoon"). The regression is the climactic manifestation of his vitality:

> he is alive there
>   in his basilisk cocoon beneath
> the one of living green; his quicksilver ferocity
>   quenched in the rustle of his fall into the sheath
> which is the shattering sudden splash that marks his
>   temporary loss.

There is a similar regression in Richard Wilbur's "The Death of a Toad," where the toad who has been caught in a power mower pours his "rare original heartsblood" back into the earth, lying "still as if he would return to stone," dying

> Toward misted and ebullient seas
> And cooling shores, toward lost Amphibia's emperies.[13]

We not only retrace the course of evolution back to inanimate nature, but we are reminded of antique statues ("the gutters of the banked and staring eyes," "the wide and antique eyes") and the death of gods. In Richard Eberhart's "The Groundhog," the speaker sees in the decaying corpse of a groundhog dead "In June, amid the golden fields," first the ferocity of the natural process, of the sun's "immense energy," and finally the pathos of the whole history of civilization which the speaker has recapitulated in his successive responses to the fact of death:

> I stood there in the whirling summer,
> My hand capped a withered heart,
> And thought of China and of Greece,
> Of Alexander in his tent;
> Of Montaigne in his tower,
> Of Saint Theresa in her wild lament.[14]

The associations in these two poems are a bit literary, a bit forced, but they illustrate all the better the climate of ideas behind the new nature poetry. They also show how animals operate in that poetry to connect inanimate nature with civilization through our current ideas about the vitality of the unconscious life and the origins of culture in the worship of animals, the contemplation of the vegetation cycle, and the killing of gods to renew the fertility of the soil.

The same psychological and anthropological knowledge can be applied to landscape. In a remarkable poem called "The Mountain," W. S. Merwin evokes the divinity of a mountain through the dispassionate accents of a modern, scientifically minded speaker who inhabits the lower slopes. "Only on the rarest occasions," the poem begins, "can one trace the rising / Slopes high enough to call them contours."

> Then
> It is with almost a shock that one recognizes
> What supposedly one had known always:
> That it is, in fact, a mountain; not merely
> This restrictive sense of nothing level, of never
> Being able to go anywhere
> But up or down, until it seems probable
> Sometimes that the slope, to be so elusive
> And yet so inescapable, must be nothing
> But ourselves: that we have grown with one
> Foot shorter than the other, and would deform

> The levellest habitat to our misshapen
Condition, as is said of certain hill creatures.

No one has seen the summit, although the attempt was at one time "a kind of holy maelstrom, Mecca / For fanatics and madmen," and there have been recent expeditions with "expensive equipment."

                                        Very few
Who set out at all seriously have
Come back. At a relatively slight distance
Above us, apparently the whole aspect and condition
Of the mountain changes completely; there is ceaseless wind
With a noise like thunder and the beating of wings.

Of those who came back, some were deaf, some blind, all "dazzled, as by a great light," those who perhaps went farthest lost the use of language and the sense of time—all of which seems "from earliest / Antiquity to have excited speculation."

One legend has it that a remote king-priest figure
Once gained the summit, spent some—to him non-sequent
But to them significant—time there, and returned
'Shining,' bearing ciphers of the arcane (which,
Translated into the common parlance, proved
To be a list of tribal taboos) like clastic
Specimens, and behaved with a glacial violence
Later construed as wisdom. This, though
Charming, does not, in the light of current endeavour,
Seem possible, even though so long ago. Yet
To corroborate this story, in the torrent
Gold has been found which even at this
Late date appears to have been powdered by hand,
And (further to confuse inquiry) several
Pediments besides, each with four sockets shaped
As though to receive the hoof of a giant statue
Of some two-toed ungulate. Legend being

What it is, there are those who still insist
He will come down again some day from the mountain.

As there are those

—and here the tension between the accumulating conviction and
the skeptical language is resolved through a transformation of the
discussion into psychological terms (myth is what happens whenever mind meets nature)—

who say it will fall on us. It
Will fall. And those who say it has already
Fallen. It has already fallen. Have we not
Seen it fall in shadow, evening after evening,
Across everything we can touch; do we not build
Our houses out of the great hard monoliths
That have crashed down from far above us? Shadows
Are not without substance, remind and predict;
And we know we live between greater commotions
Than any we can describe. But, most important:
Since this, though we know so little of it, is
All we know, is it not whatever it makes us
Believe of it—even the old woman
Who laughs, pointing, and says that the clouds across
Its face are wings of seraphim? Even the young
Man who, standing on it, declares it is not
There at all. He stands with one leg habitually
Bent, to keep from falling, as though he had grown
That way, as is said of certain hill creatures.[15]

The mountain is divine in the same sense as Marianne Moore's
cobra in "Snakes, Mongooses." Whatever we think the mountain
is, its irreducible otherness remains; and the cobra's perfect singleness of line, as it stands up from the snake-charmer's basket, anni-
hilates distinctions, showing "that when intelligence in its pure
form / has embarked on a train of thought which is unproductive, /
it will come back"—back to the otherness of reality. These intui-

tions of reality are like Frost's "dark wood," except that they involve, too, a distinct sense of the past, and therefore of the present. Since they stimulate us to apply all we know of current ideas, they bring out into the open what must be, I suppose, the ultimate subject of nature poetry—the divinity in nature.

The history of nature poetry is in a sense recapitulated in Wallace Stevens's lovely meditation, "Sunday Morning." The consistent water imagery suggests that the modern cosmopolitan lady ought, to make the poem properly meditative-descriptive, to be looking out over water as she lounges late of a sunny Sunday morning, aware that she is not after all in church. Certain tropical accouterments, "coffee and oranges,"

> And the green freedom of a cockatoo
> Upon a rug mingle to dissipate
> The holy hush of ancient sacrifice

but remind her, too, of sacrifices more ancient still than Christ's:

> The pungent oranges and bright, green wings
> Seem things in some procession of the dead,
> Winding across wide water, without sound.

"Why should she give her bounty to the dead?" she asks. "Divinity must live within herself: / Passions of rain, or moods in falling snow." Thus she comes past the rejection of Christianity to the transcendentalism of romantic nature poetry with its moments of private insight. She remembers the alienation of religion from nature with sky-gods like Jove, and how Christianity brought God back to earth again—although it bequeathed the uneasy question whether earth was to be brought to heaven or heaven to earth. Nature is her paradise; no, better than paradise. For death makes the difference, "is the mother of beauty," gives the outlet to imagination, the savor to life.

Awareness of death leads to a vision of *communal* nature worship, with this difference from ancient rites—that in the new

religion of earth the sun would be worshipped not as a god, but
for itself:

> Supple and turbulent, a ring of men
> Shall chant in orgy on a summer morn
> Their boisterous devotion to the sun,
> Not as a god, but as a god might be,
> Naked among them, like a savage source.

It is when we see nature as a source of both life and death that appreciation turns into worship. The natural cycle is the source of all
religions:

> They shall know well the heavenly fellowship
> Of men that perish and of summer morn.
> And whence they came and whither they shall go
> The dew upon their feet shall manifest.

In the final section, Stevens not only completes his poem by
returning us to the water and answering the question he raised
about Christianity, he also completes his history of nature poetry.

> She hears, upon that water without sound,
> A voice that cries, "The tomb in Palestine
> Is not the porch of spirits lingering.
> It is the grave of Jesus, where he lay."

In terms of its own supernatural claims, Christianity is dead; but
after all that has been said in the poem we must understand, too,
that as the worship of the dead god, of the natural cycle, Christianity is part of an inherent religion that always has lived and always will live. The poem ends with one of the very best passages
of modern American nature poetry, a passage which, deriving its
poignancy from the strength of its resistance to the pathetic fallacy, expresses perfectly the sense in which, with what we now
know about the unconscious life of man and nature, we can feel
that the world both is and is not God-abandoned.

We live in an old chaos of the sun,
Or old dependency of day and night,
Or island solitude, unsponsored, free,
Of that wide water, inescapable.
Deer walk upon our mountains, and the quail
Whistle about us their spontaneous cries;
Sweet berries ripen in the wilderness;
And, in the isolation of the sky,
At evening, casual flocks of pigeons make
Ambiguous undulations as they sink,
Downward to darkness, on extended wings.

Those "ambiguous undulations" are the point where nature poetry comes full circle from the rejection of the old religion of nature to the discovery of an inevitably re-emerging religion of nature at the source of things.

A
NEW LOOK
AT
E. M. FORSTER

To those of us who admire E. M. Forster, all five of his novels exhibit his special charm and are therefore indispensable. Yet future readers who are not specialists in English literature may remember him for only one novel, *Passage to India*. With time Forster's last novel, published in 1924, increasingly detaches itself from the rest of his work as incommensurably major.

Wilfred Stone, in *The Cave and the Mountain: A Study of E. M. Forster* (1966), shows the advantage of such critical hindsight—an advantage over Lionel Trilling who, in his brilliant introductory study of 1943, rated *Howard's End* highest—in that Stone treats all Forster's work in order to display *Passage* as a culmination. In this, the biggest and most thoroughly researched book we have so far had on Forster, Stone makes us realize how unpredictable and incalculable was the leap of imagination that led to *Passage*. Forster published his first four novels between 1905 and 1910, but waited fourteen years to publish *Passage*, which he began during his first visit to India in 1912–1913. Stone describes these intervening years as a spiritual passage eastward—accomplished through Forster's residence in Egypt (especially Alexandria) about which he wrote three nonfiction books, and finally in India where he returned in 1921. Forster couldn't *write* the novel, however, until he got back to England.

Stone helps us understand why Forster has written no fiction since *Passage to India;* for he shows how in *Passage* Forster answers all the questions posed in the earlier work, and indeed enlarges the questions themselves. Given Forster's starting point in turn-of-the-century liberalism and aestheticism, he says in *Passage* all he had to say and all perhaps that there is to say. Since then, he has wisely preferred writing criticism and biography to writing inferior fiction.

Actually, Forster has written two masterpieces—his last novel and his first, *Where Angels Fear to Tread. Angels* is on a much smaller scale than *Passage;* it is a perfect little comedy of manners. Such success at first try shows that Forster's talent is essentially comic; and criticism, which is better suited to talk about the ideas and symbols in the novels, has never done justice to their lightness and charm. Except for George Eliot in her lighter moments, Forster is the only English novelist in whom one can discern another Jane Austen. The question is why Forster was not content to go on writing comedy.

The answer is that no writer of integrity, standing this side of the romantic and relativistic nineteenth century, can write for long like Jane Austen. To write like her, a novelist has to believe in his society, believe that its norms represent some ultimate truth and that the job of comedy is to correct deviations from the norms. Forster's characters have, instead, to be judged and to work out their destinies through shifting and inadequate standards. That is why Forster takes a comparative attitude toward cultures, and why his more enlightened characters work out their destinies between cultures. The lack of valid standards leads to a complex irony that criticizes not only English middle-class values, but the alternatives as well, and the very characters who seek the alternatives. The lack of standards leads also to concern with a mystical reality behind the shifting social surfaces. Hence the romantic emphasis on nature and imaginative apprehension, that assorts so oddly with the witty notation of manners. Hence Forster's attempt to combine comedy with prophecy or vision.

The characteristic combinations of Forster's art are most complex in *Passage*, which compares three cultures—West European Christian, Indian Moslem, and Indian Hindu—as decreasingly inadequate representations of the unmeaning echo in the Marabar Caves and Mrs. Moore's imaginative apprehension of the echo. The European culture stands for will and order; the Moslem for emotion and erotic love; the Hindu for a disorder and impassivity that comes closest to representing a comprehensiveness that dissolves distinctions and manifests itself as nothingness. Thus the *metaphysical* adequacy of Hinduism, especially for the modern scientific view of the world, the fact that Hinduism operates way beyond good and evil, order and disorder, exclusiveness and inclusiveness, makes it for all *practical* purposes the most inadequate of the three cultures. Neither Forster nor his hero, Fielding, can finally accept it—though they see that it takes into account more of reality than "poor talkative little Christianity" with its attempt to draw an ethical and rationalistic pattern from the most recent history of only one species, man, in the vast round of animate and inanimate nature.

A far simpler book, *Where Angela Fear to Tread* compares only two cultures—England, standing for will and order, and Italy, standing for emotion and erotic love. By reference to comic stereotypes, Forster quickly sketches in the manners of Sawston, upper middle-class English suburbia, and throws them into comic juxtaposition to the manners of San Gimignano (here called Monteriano), the almost perfectly preserved thirteenth-century town near Siena. Haughty old Mrs. Herriton of Sawston sends her aesthetical son, Philip, out to rescue Lilia, the giddy widow of her dead son, from an impending marriage to "Italian nobility" (Mrs. Herriton

snorts at the "fatuous vulgarity" of that phrase in the telegram
from Italy). Our laughter proceeds from recollection of other comedies about snobs; so that we know how to respond when Philip
on arriving learns, "to his personal disgust and pain," that what
Lilia has in fact married is of all things the son of a dentist! "A
dentist! A dentist at Monteriano. A dentist in fairyland! False
teeth and laughing gas and the tilting chair at a place which knew
the Etruscan League, and the Pax Romana, and Alaric himself. . . ." [1]

Yet this is another order of snobbery that takes us beyond the
external comedy of national and class distinctions. For Philip, unlike his mother and sister, Harriet, has the tourist's attitude and rejects Gino as betraying Philip's ideal of Italy. The thing, however,
that ties all the Herritons and Lilia and Caroline Abbott, the sensitive spinster who chaperoned Lilia in Italy, is what Forster in his
essay, "Notes on the English Character," has called the "undeveloped heart." [2] Forster transforms the traditional comedy of manners to dramatize the conflict between English middle-class manners of the undeveloped heart and Italian manners of authenticity.
The Italian manners belong to no class (Gino does not behave
like an Italian bourgeois); they have been idealized out of the ob-
servable natural courtesy of guides and servants.

We see the manners of the undeveloped heart in the ludicrous
contrast between Monteriano and the picture of Harriet squeezing
out her sponges, as, after Lilia's death, she prepares dutifully and
with distaste to accompany Philip on a second mission to the
lovely old Tuscan town—this time to rescue Lilia's baby from the
Italian cad, Gino. Philip and Caroline are better, but even they violate Italy by refusing to see it as it is, by using it as a romantic escape from the social grooves. (Lilia married Gino to escape, then
learned to her sorrow that Italy has its own social grooves.) There
are in this and the other novels three grades of Englishmen—the
Philistines, who never see beyond middle-class values, the tourists

or sensitives who try to break away but can't quite, and the authentic people who either are or become what they ought to be.

By the standards of authenticity, the Herritons are vulgar in the compact they make to keep secret the existence of Lilia's son and in their purpose, once the secret is out, to procure the baby just to preserve their good name. Even the heroine, Caroline Abbott, is vulgar in attempting to buy the baby in order to assuage her conscience for having encouraged Lilia to marry Gino (she did so to satisfy vicariously her own unacknowledged attraction to him). Gino, for all his coarsely avowed fortune-hunting (coarseness reveals, vulgarity conceals—says Forster in *Longest Journey*), never for a moment considers their offers. We can never be sure about Gino's motives, but his actions are somehow right—though without moral pretension.

Gino is authentic because he is like Italy itself a vital and attractive mixture of "Beauty, evil, charm, vulgarity, mystery." Caroline, who is sure Gino is not fit to bring up the baby, learns from him "the terrible truth, that wicked people are capable of love." Gino's relation to his son is justified by his grasp of a biological mystery Miss Abbott cannot understand—the sense that through his son "physical and spiritual life may stream out of him forever." [3]

Gino is an erotic force, the only *man* in the book, since Philip is an aesthetical eunuch. Gino—who is irresistibly attractive to Lilia, Caroline and Philip, even when they disapprove of him—stands a little way beyond good and evil, pointing toward the romantic erotic force of Dr. Aziz in *Passage* and the unmeaning erotic force of the caves. Forster has worked throughout his career, notably in the short stories, to evoke such a force (his first story, "The Story of a Panic," is about a beautiful and destructive manifestation of Pan); yet in the novels the erotic force is successfully evoked only here and in *Passage*. It is only the sensitive English people, capable of venturing a few steps beyond the moral categories, who can apprehend the erotic force; but since even they must tamper, must impose their moralizing and transcendentalizing wills, the experience turns destructive. In transcendentalizing Italy and Gino, Philip and Caroline practice a destructiveness that differs only in subtlety from the destructiveness of Harriet, who finally kidnaps the baby which gets killed in an accident.

In the final scene, where we learn that Caroline loves Gino but will do nothing about it and that Philip thinks he loves Caroline but is relieved, after her confession about Gino, that he need do nothing about it, in this scene we understand why Forster had to go beyond comedy of manners. For the failure here is too psychological, and too intimatcly determined not only by place and class but by the historical moment, to be capable of any solution at all, let alone a solution expressed as a shift to "good" manners or well-balanced behavior. As in *Passage*, the contrast is not only between English character and that of another country, but between the distinctively modern and the traditional in character. *Angels* brings comedy up against its limits in the hopelessness of the modern condition, but never itself advances into prophecy or the poetical.

Forster's subsequent concern with comedy and prophecy explains the distinction he makes, in *Aspects of the Novel* (1927), between "flat" and "round" characters. Flat characters are the characters out of old-fashioned comedy who, like the female Herritons, are solidly entrenched in a social order and display one or two leading traits deriving from their position in that order. But the sensitive characters, who question the code, find their identities in an inner life at odds with the social order and "continually threaten to achieve roundness." To the extent that they do achieve roundness, our view of them becomes psychological and empathic rather than comic. The two principal influences on Forster arc Jane Austen and Proust. From Jane Austen, Forster has said, he learned "the possibilities of domestic humor," and from Proust, "ways of looking at character . . . the modern subconscious way." [4]

Although Stone does not give sufficient credit to *Angels* (he does not recognize its purely comic achievement because he gives more attention to Philip and his problems, treats him as "rounder," than the novel warrants), he is acute on the limitations of the three subsequent novels. In one of his many perceptive summations, Stone says that "Forster's fiction is essentially an experiment in self-confidence. One after another his main characters, like so many groundhogs, poke their heads out of their sanctuaries to see whether it is safe to emerge further." [5] The sanctuaries are the ivory towers of pure speculation and sensibility that Forster inhabited among his intellectual friends in Cambridge and later Bloomsbury. If we add the notion that Forster was also finding out how far it was safe to emerge from the sanctuary of comedy, we have a good key to the subsequent novels. In *The Longest Journey* (1907), his most purely poetical and least successful novel, he emerges very far from comedy—attempting an internal drama of failed idealism, a kind of *Alastor*, for which like Shelley himself he has not found an adequate machinery of events. He retreats in *A Room with a View* (1908), writing what he himself calls his "nicest" book, a sentimental comedy that slyly evades the modern condition. He emerges again in *Howard's End* (1910), where in taking his first really serious look at English society, he writes his most intelligent novel except for *Passage*. But even *Howard's End* conducts us back to a sanctuary.

In emerging from Cambridge, the anti-hero of *Longest Journey*, lame, sensitive, self-accusing Rickie Elliot moves into social reality by marrying Agnes and taking a job teaching at the snobbish Sawston Public School where her odious brother Herbert is a Master. Although the general tone is that of an ironical realism that sees around moral questions, all Rickie's antagonists, his wife, brother-in-law and brutal father, show up as melodramatically villainous. Forster is clearly paying off old personal scores—which is to say that he is uncertain about his distance from Rickie. Rickie comes out, therefore, as more of a sap than the author can have intended.

Forster fails also in his characterization of Rickie's anti-self, his illegitimate half-brother, Stephen Wonham. Stephen is intended to be a hero and a natural man. But his naturalness is never a significant force, because it is not displayed as an erotic force. Compared to Gino, Stephen is curiously emasculate and 'pure'—a muscular Peter Pan. If erotic force were a reality in this novel, we would be able to understand why for Rickie the acknowledgment of Stephen as his brother is a shattering initiation into reality. We would understand that it is the erotic revelation about his mother, and not simply preference for her over his father, that causes Rickie to faint when he learns that Stephen is not, as he had automatically assumed, the bastard of his hated father but of his beloved mother. We would understand why Rickie's aunt takes him, when she breaks the news of his relation to Stephen, to the center of the Cadbury Rings, a double circle of ancient earthworks—which is, unlike the dell at Cambridge where Rickie liked to retreat, an enclosure at the heart of reality, a kind of womb of England. Stone connects the symbolism of enclosures, throughout Forster's work, with the caves in *Passage* and with the symbolism of Hindu temples from which *The Cave and the Mountain* derives its title.[6]

Partly this is a Shelleyan story, exalting idealism and Platonic friendships over the possessiveness of sexual love (hence the title, deriving from Shelley's *Epipsychidion*). Partly it is a Laurentian novel *manqué*, exalting nature and the life force without explicitly exalting sexuality. The conflict between the Cambridge ivory tower and the social reality of Sawston is supposed to be subsumed in Wiltshire—the county which is, we are told, the quintessence of English landscape—and in an authentically English type that emerges from this landscape. Stephen seems at times to be this authentic type, but at other times he falls short because of his brutality. He certainly falls short of his father, an educated farmer who emerges as unequivocally authentic—but in a passage too short to make much impression. This part of the novel is not successful.

The successful story is the *Bildungsroman*, the story of how Rickie, the young writer, discovers his true self and his true vocation by finally recognizing his brother. But in abandoning Agnes, whom he had idealized, for Stephen, Rickie can only swing from one overblown ideal to another. Rickie transcendentalizes Stephen (Forster himself sometimes participates in the process and is sometimes ironical about it), when he thinks of his alliance with him as a decision to "trust the earth."

Because Rickie has never *seen* Stephen as he is in himself, he is extravagantly disillusioned when Stepehen gets dead drunk, thus breaking a promise not to drink for a few days. In dying to save Stephen's life, Rickie finally makes contact with reality because he sacrifices his life for a failed ideal—for Stephen lying drunk in the path of an oncoming train. Although there are no heroics in Rickie's *action*, he dies with the old overblown nonsense on his lips when he whispers that he ought to have bewared of "the earth," meaning Stephen.[7] It is just such ironical qualification of even intense moments that marks Forster at his best. And, indeed, there is in this novel so much finely ironical intelligence coupled with tender intimacy as to endear it, in spite of its faults, to Forster's admirers—especially since it is a seedbed of his subsequent work.

In *A Room with a View*, the contrast is again between Sawston and Italy (Part One, the Italian part, was written at the same time as *Angels*); but Italy, in this novel, is not a serious cultural alternative. It is a pastoral setting where Englishmen on holiday can find their heart's desire, aided by Italians who are the shepherds and nymphs of pastoral masquerading as guides and other attendants upon tourists.

For Lucy Honeychurch, the heroine, there is no question of cultural migration; her problem is whether she dares marry an Englishman, one notch below her on the middle-class scale, whose father is an outspokenly atheistical socialist. Old Mr. Emerson offends because his manners are all too good—benevolently democratic, free of affectation and snobbery. It is clear from the start that the Emersons pose no real threat to Sawston and that when Lucy, after the inevitable wrong engagement to a coxcomb, finally follows her own heart and good sense and marries George Emerson, the social order will be strengthened. The only distinctively modern element in the book is the psychological treatment of Lucy's puritanically repressed cousin and chaperone, who is vicariously involved in her relation with George. But Charlotte's story is treated lightly so as not to destroy the gossamer workmanship of *Room*. As a piece of flimflam, *Room* is successful and might be considered Forster's holiday before he undertakes his most earnest novel, *Howard's End*.

In *Howard's End*, Forster finally writes about metropolitan intellectuals, people like his Bloomsbury friends, who are liberals, aesthetes, 'tourists.' I say finally though Forster has written all along about this position, which is his own (he might be called the novelist of the tourist mentality; a reader of guidebooks, he has himself written a guide to Alexandria). Up till now, however, the real loyalties of his characters have been to class and country, even if they showed a tourist's appreciation of Italy. The upper middle-class Schlegel sisters of *Howard's End*, instead, feel classless and therefore alienated from society. It is a sign of their alienation that they are half-foreign—daughters of a German idealist who left his country when he felt it had abandoned its own best principles.

The Schlegel sisters are gently satirized for moving in that "aura of self-congratulation" which Lionel Trilling finds characteristic of liberal intellectuals.[8] They take a tourist's attitude toward England in their desire to "connect" with it—a desire no one committed to some social niche would feel. Helen Schlegel is thrilled by the rich business family, the Wilcoxes, because they challenge her stand on public issues when they call "Equality . . . nonsense . . . Art and Literature . . . nonsense." Margaret Schlegel delights in the gaucheries of the low middle-class clerk, Leonard Bast, because she is moved by his attempt to improve himself through self-education and culture. Later, the sisters switch allegiances. Margaret marries the Wilcox father; and Helen, out of class guilt, gives herself to Leonard and has a child by him to atone for the economic injury Mr. Wilcox has done him. But since these connections with such impossible men are not accounted for by erotic infatuation (eros is not a reality in this book), they can only be taken allegorically.

Allegorically, the connections represent attempts to put together an original cultural unity represented by the first Mrs. Wilcox and the farmhouse, Howard's End, that has come down to her through her family. (All the other houses in the book are rented.) The elderly Ruth Wilcox is Forster's first draft of his greatest portrayal, the elderly Mrs. Moore of *Passage*. Until now, Forster's authentic characters have been men who exert force through vitality. With Ruth Wilcox, he portrays authenticity through negative qualities —passivity and stillness. She is the most memorable character in *Howard's End*, for she carries her own atmosphere with her; she is not just another character, she is another order of existence altogether. Although failing in health, she seems stronger than her modern-minded husband and children, because she is rooted in *Howard's End*, which is in turn rooted in the landscape. This rootedness makes her, though she is not clever like the Schlegels' intellectual friends, thoroughly cultured, an aristocrat.

> She seemed to belong not to the young people and their motor, but to the house, and to the tree that overshadowed it. One knew that she worshipped the past, and that the instinctive wisdom the past alone can bestow had descended upon her—that wisdom to which we give the clumsy name of aristocracy. High-born she might not be. But assuredly she cared about her ancestors, and let them help her.

Mrs. Wilcox, on her deathbed, leaves Howard's End to Margaret in an unsigned note that the Wilcoxes destroy. This raises the book's central question. Like Wiltshire in *Longest Journey*, Howard's End is traditional England. And the question is: Who shall inherit England—the Philistine guardians of her material wealth, who are governed by self-interest; or the disinterested guardians of her culture, who transcend the clash of class interests by an appeal to principles, to the best that has been thought and said? I borrow terms from Matthew Arnold to show that *Howard's End* dramatizes Arnold's idea of culture. When Margaret says "Only connect!"—the phrase is the book's epigraph—"Only connect the prose and the passion," she is aspiring toward that Unity of Being for which Arnold praises Sophocles, whom "Business could not make dull, nor Passion wild: / Who saw life steadily, and saw it whole." [9] But Forster's idea of culture derives also from the larger romantic tradition that sees culture as reaching perfection, both in society and the individual, at that point where it coincides with nature, where culture shows forth as man's equivalent for nature.

It is allegorically right that Margaret, who has tried to breach the modern gap between business and passion, should eventually acquire Howard's End by marrying Mr. Wilcox. Yet the tableau at the end is less encouraging than Forster seems to realize. Howard's End is inhabited by Margaret and Helen, with Helen's illegitimate baby boy. The eldest Wilcox son is in prison for having helped bring on Leonard Bast's death by beating him up; Mr. Wilcox is a broken man dependent on Margaret for guidance, because he has had no inner ballast with which to withstand catastrophe. The implication is that if England is to have culture, it must be in the hands of women. Nor is Forster being ironical about the ending; for his hopes are apparently on Helen's son, who will inherit Howard's End. But what chance has Helen's son, raised in such a household, not to turn out like the Schlegel brother, Tibby, a cultivated dishrag of a man?

For all its fascinating play of ideas, *Howard's End* can be criticized for the dead stretches when characters and events are merely at the service of the ideas, and for the inept scenes dealing with Leonard Bast and his sluttish wife. (Forster admitted he knew nothing about the home life of such people.[10] He cannot do lower-class characters unless they are exotic enough to be turned into symbols of natural force—like his Italian guides, or the naked Untouchable who moves the fan in the courtroom in *Passage.*) But the main objection is Stone's when he criticizes Forster's evasiveness in making women his experimenters in excursion, and in presenting finally "a moral failure as a triumph." [11] The idea of culture as feminine is imbedded in Anglo-Saxon, as it is not in Latin, countries. But the idea is also a peculiarity of Forster and of his homosexual Cambridge friend, G. Lowes Dickinson, about whom Forster has written a biography. It is the spinsterish fastidiousness of Forster's comedy that reminds us of Jane Austen; but the old-maid quality can, when it shows forth seriously, mar his work.

To understand Forster's intellectual milieu, one has to understand Dickinson, the Cambridge don who most influenced Forster. Dickinson was a latter-day Shelley, a Shelley gone sedentary and soft, but still it was through Dickinson's sentimental Hellenism, his Platonic mysticism distrustful of religious creeds, his opposition to imperialism and war, his exaltation of friendship, that Forster imbibed the spirit of idealism that provides one pole in the dialectic of his novels. One has also to understand the Cambridge "set," Tennyson's society of the Apostles, to which Forster and Dickinson belonged. In Tennyson's time, the Apostles avoided the opposing dogmas of Christian orthodoxy and Utilitarianism through a romantic position that yielded religious intensity without theology. In Forster's time, the Apostles opposed to the latest dogmas a frankly aesthetic attitude and an extravagant faith in the sanctity of the individual. It was from these Apostles, regathered in

London, that the original Bloomsbury Group drew most of its members. For Bloomsbury (of which Forster was a fringe member), all creeds, especially political creeds, were suspect; ideas in action were crude. All that mattered was the refinement of individual sensibility through art and personal relations.

Both Stone and Frederick Crews, in his book on Forster, trace the nineteenth-century background to Forster's intellectual position—showing how as great-grandson of the Evangelical and Utilitarian M.P. Henry Thornton of Clapham, Forster has made the characteristic century-long migration of English liberal intellectuals from Clapham to Bloomsbury. Clapham, center of the upper middle-class intellectual elite of the early nineteenth century, believed, as I have explained in "The Victorian Idea of Culture," in reform, moral action and laissez-faire economics. Their descendants, as represented by Bloomsbury and *The Independent Review* of which Dickinson was a founder, cared only for a laissez-faire of the spirit and to achieve that—says Crews in his revealing chapter on Forster's liberalism—were ready to accept "collectivist legislation" as "positively necessary to prevent society from exercising a tyranny of fortune and opinion over the individual." In this, says Crews, they were following the evolution of English liberalism out of the later John Stuart Mill.[12] They were also, I would add, in their suspicion of action and their respect only for a liberalism of ideas, following Matthew Arnold. They were certainly following Arnold in treating politics as a branch of culture. In the liberalism of *The Independent Review*, we saw, says Forster, "avenues opening into literature, philosophy, human relationships. . . . Can you imagine decency touched with poetry?" [13]

But the paeans to the individual really covered up secret misgivings that the individual was soon to count for nothing. "The people I respect most," writes Forster in *Two Cheers for Democracy*, "behave as if they were immortal and as if society was eternal. Both assumptions are false: both of them must be accepted as true if we are to go on eating and working and loving, and are to keep open a few breathing holes for the human spirit." [14] Crews sees this "combination of pessimism and idealism" as characteristic of Forster's novels. The combination is especially characteristic of *Passage to India,* and accounts for its continuing relevance.

To appreciate Forster's achievement in *Passage to India,* we have to roll up into this last novel not only his earlier writings, but the whole liberal tradition with all the questions it has bequeathed us. What advance does *Passage* make over the earlier novels? It is set in a universe so much larger as to change our perspective toward human affairs and therefore the meaning of the questions raised, though they are ostensibly the same. We have seen how from the start Forster sets his comedies in a natural world beyond good and evil. India showed him, however, that even his natural settings were too domestic and pretty, and led to the false expectation of an answer to moral questions since such questions occurred in a world that at least aesthetically made sense.

India, we are told in *Passage,* is not beautiful. It is not romantic, for it is a "muddle" not a "mystery." Mystery promises an answer, and romanticism is concerned with the adumbrations of order to be found in beauty and mystery. India, in its social and historical muddle and in its formless landscape, is developed as a powerful symbol of unknowable reality.

The perspective of *Passage* is established in sentences like this: "It matters so little to the majority of living beings what the minority, that calls itself human, desires or decides." Not only are human affairs seen in the perspective of the whole animal world, but all of life is seen as an almost imperceptible instant in the vast and timeless story of inanimate nature.

> The high places of Dravidia have been land since land began, and have seen on the one side the sinking of a continent that joined them to Africa, and on the other the upheaval of the Himalayas from a sea. They are older than anything in the world. No water has ever covered them, and the sun who has watched them for countless aeons may still discern in their

outlines forms that were his before our globe was torn from his bosom. If flesh of the sun's flesh is to be touched anywhere, it is here, among the incredible antiquity of these hills. . . . To call them "uncanny" suggests ghosts, and they are older than all spirit.[15]

Here are to be found the Marabar Caves, so featureless, so alike and yet so unlike anything else in the world that they cannot be talked about.

Approaching the Marabar on the picnic arranged by Dr. Aziz, the English hark back nostalgically to Grasmere with its recollections of Wordsworth and his so different view of nature. " 'Ah, dearest Grasmere!' Its little lakes and mountains were beloved by them all. Romantic yet manageable, it sprang from a kindlier planet." Even the cultured skepticism that unites Fielding and Adela Quested seems too romantic and manageable to be adequate to the reality projected in this novel.

> When they agreed, "I want to go on living a bit," or, "I don't believe in God," the words were followed by a curious back wash as though the universe had displaced itself to fill up a tiny void, or as though they had seen their own gestures from an immense height—dwarfs talking, shaking hands and assuring each other that they stood on the same footing of insight.

It is in these vast interstellar spaces that the old Forster themes are played out—the comedy of manners, the romantic belief in experience and personal relations, the liberal search for a just political order. The morally annihilating effect of so much space-time is projected through the echo in the cave that throws Mrs. Moore into a panic. The echo, she recalls,

> had managed to murmur, "Pathos, piety, courage—they exist, but are identical, and so is filth. Everything exists, nothing has value." If one had spoken vileness in that place, or quoted lofty poetry, the comment would have been the same—"ouboum." . . . suddenly, at the edge of her mind, Religion appeared, poor little talkative Christianity, and she knew that all its divine words from "Let there be Light" to "It is finished" only amounted to "boum."

In the comic misunderstandings that lead, at Fielding's tea party in Chapter VII, to the organizing of the fatal picnic, we see how comedy of manners turns into something else. The picnic gets organized because Adela has made the mistake of taking literally Dr. Aziz's invitation to visit him. Dr. Aziz, thinking with horror of his wretched bungalow, suggests that the party come as his guests, instead, to the Marabar Caves. It then turns out comically that Aziz has himself never been there; and when he tries to get Professor Godbole to explain why the caves are extraordinary, the Brahman can only say what they are not. Listening to the friendly dialogue, Adela did not realize "that the comparatively simple mind of the Mohammedan was encountering Ancient Night." Suddenly, the comic muddle turns symbolic.

Comedy returns with the entrance of Ronny, the priggish official who is Mrs. Moore's son and the man Adela has come to India to marry. Ronny's bad manners in disapproving of Adela's company unnerves Aziz, who responds with an aggressive over-familiarity that confirms Anglo-Indian prejudices. " 'What should have upset his [Aziz's] precious nerves? . . . Well, it's nothing I've said,' " says Ronny with sublime obtuseness. " 'I never even spoke to him.' " The party breaks up, the good manners of the salutations contrasting with the bad feeling. But then, Adela's merely polite remark to Godbole, " 'It's a shame we never heard you sing,' " brings back the symbolism of Ancient Night. For Godbole begins to sing, a tuneless song about a milkmaiden who repeatedly asks the god Krishna to come, but the god refuses. " 'But He comes in some other song, I hope?' " asks Mrs. Moore, hoping for a rationale. " 'He neglects to come,' " is the reply.[16]

All the values of the novel are in this scene, which points toward the central episode of the cave. We see how Aziz gets involved in the relation of Adela and Ronny; so that Adela, who wanders into a cave thinking of Ronny's lack of attractiveness, has given back to her by the cave her own sense of Aziz's attractiveness when she imagines he has followed her inside to attack her. In the ensuing scandal and trial, Aziz seems again to have confirmed the worst Anglo-Indian prejudices. Most important, we see already in this scene the breakdown of amity through the upsurge of fundamental feelings.

Part I, "Mosque," to which the scene belongs, is about the attempt to breach the gap between India and England through the friendship of enlightened individuals—notably the friendship of Aziz with Fielding and Mrs. Moore. Part II, "Caves," is about the breakdown of this Apollonian hope before irrational forces. All the relations of Part I dissolve. Mrs. Moore, who after her experience in the cave loses interest in people and moral issues, makes no move to help Aziz, but starts back to England, dying on the way. Adela and Ronny break up; she returns to England. Aziz, after the case has been dismissed, becomes suspicious of Fielding's motives in dissuading him from suing Adela; he suspects Fielding of intending to marry her. Fielding returns to England.

Part III, "Temple," attempts a new synthesis. It takes place in a Hindu principality, where Godbole is now Minister of Education and Aziz, out of disgust with British India, has taken a post as court physician. The section opens with a long, masterful description of the festival celebrating the birth of Krishna. The festival reminds us of Christmas, showing the universality of the myth. But the differences are even more important. "They did not one thing which the non-Hindu would feel dramatically correct; this approaching triumph of India was a muddle (as we call it), a frustration of reason and form." [17]

Part III has puzzled many critics; some have even judged it a letdown, whereas the book moves most boldly forward in Part III. For to the book's central question, the conflict between reality and justice, Forster is offering the Hindu answer—the mythical view of life. One remembers Yeats's remark that his mythical system helped him "to hold in a single thought reality and justice." [18] Through myth, Forster tells us, "the human spirit had tried by a desperate contortion to ravish the unknown, flinging down science and history in the struggle, yes, beauty herself." Myth, with its muddle, comes as close as expression can to rendering accessible the formlessness of reality. Myth is the human equivalent to the natural reality of the caves.

The festival is curiously efficacious. For it is there, in an atmosphere "thick with religion and rain," that Aziz and Fielding are reconciled and Aziz's bond with Mrs. Moore renewed through her children, Ralph and Stella (Aziz learns that Fielding has married Stella, not Adela). In the same way, Mrs. Moore becomes a potent force in the novel after she breaks through, in the experience of the cave, to a mentality like Godbole's, to the mythical mentality. Because she refuses to take a stand based on the distinction between good and evil, she does not assail people from outside but takes them over from inside. She becomes part of the echo that haunts Adela's mind, causing her finally to withdraw charges against Aziz; she becomes a goddess to the Hindu mob, who imagine she was killed because she wanted to save an Indian; she retains her hold on Aziz's affection, though she has done less than Fielding and Adela to save him. Because of Mrs. Moore, Fielding gets married; and Aziz's reconciliation with Fielding begins with his sympathy for Ralph Moore, who is like his mother "Oriental" in spirit.

But we do not, as in Part I, make the mistake of supposing that success in one sphere can change matters in another. Although at the end Fielding and Aziz are horseback-riding together, we see that they have moved apart politically. Fielding now finds things to be said for British imperialism; while Aziz is fanatically anti-British.

> "We shall get rid of you, yes, we shall drive every blasted Englishman into the sea, and then"—he rode against him furiously—"and then," he concluded, half kissing him, "you and I shall be friends."
>
> "Why can't we be friends now?" said the other, holding him affectionately. "It's what I want. It's what you want."
>
> But the horses didn't want it—they swerved apart; the earth

didn't want it, sending up rocks through which riders must
pass single file. . . .[19]

Personal settlements do not change political and natural reality.

Yet I cannot agree with Frederick Crews that the conclusion is
entirely negative and hopeless. There is at the end the fortifying
pleasure of seeing all things in their due place, of understanding
the validity of things because we understand the limits of their validity. Nor is the vision of reality entirely nihilistic. Although we
cannot read Forster's symbolism by reference to Hindu theology,
for he takes what he wants from Hinduism, the lesson of the caves
is not, as Crews thinks, *anti*-Hindu. Mrs. Moore emerges from the
caves as in effect a positive, beneficent force. The very void projected by the echo is a spiritual presence. It is in just such "espaces
infinis" as filled Pascal with awe that the modern sensibility finds
spirit. "Where there is nothing, where there is nothing—" says
Yeats, "there is God!" [20]

Stone catches perfectly the mood of Part III when he speaks of
its "mud-bespattered hilarity" (the festival is full of horseplay; the
English party take a redemptive spill in the river when they row
out to view the festival).

> To say that "God so loved the world that he took monkey's
> flesh upon him" suggests a new mood of spiritual gusto. . . .
> Redemption is of the earth, earthy, and of the water, watery;
> it is full of filth and disorder, yet Forster mixes in it with joy.
> It almost seems that prophecy and a sense of humor may not,
> after all, be utterly incompatible.[21]

One might go farther and say that the two necessarily go together when the vision is complete. For one is reminded of
Thomas Mann's observations, in "Freud and the Future," that the
mythical view is the complete, mature view and is characteristically
"blithe." But this does not make *Passage* itself a myth; for to offer
myth as a solution is to take a critical stance outside myth—a critical stance appropriate to a great novel, a novel already established
as a twentieth-century English classic.

MAILER'S
NEW
STYLE

Norman Mailer is a most irritating author to write about. His public image is entirely too powerful and unattractive; and his ideas, as stated in his essays, are often nonsensical (his mystique of the apocalyptic orgasm or of the spiritual significance of cancer) and sometimes intolerable (his glorification of Hip criminality). The result is that people have not taken his recent novels seriously enough. Since his image is by now better known than his novels, people like the Sunday *Times* reviewer of *Why Are We in Vietnam?* are apt to write him off as belonging more to the history of publicity than to the history of literature. And the success of his political writings since the novels—*Miami and the Siege of Chicago* and *Armies of the Night* (1968)—has only made people say he is better as journalist than novelist.[1]

Yet if we forget the public image and read through the five novels, we find that Mailer's ideas are fruitful for his fiction and that he has as much artistic integrity as anyone writing today. First of all he has refused to capitalize on the spectacular success of his first novel, *The Naked and the Dead* (1948). Having at twenty-five triumphed in the received realistic style of American social-consciousness fiction, Mailer has been working ever since at finding a new style. It was not until 1965, the year *American Dream* came out in book form, and 1967, the year of *Why Are We in Vietnam?*, that he finally broke through to a style new enough to offend many of the reviewers.

"The realistic literature," said Mailer in a paper of 1965, "had never caught up with the rate of change in American life, indeed it had fallen further and further behind, and the novel gave up any desire to be a creation equal to the phenomenon of the country itself; it settled for being a metaphor." Novelists were "no longer writing about the beast but, as in the case of Hemingway (if we are to take the best of this), about the paw of the beast, or in Faulkner about the dreams of the beast." [2]

Mailer's whole attempt in his second novel, *Barbary Shore* (1951), is to turn fiction into metaphor, indeed into an allegory of the beast's political dreams. To achieve allegory, Mailer abandons scope. Whereas *Naked* portrays the Pacific campaign of World War II and the American society behind it, *Barbary Shore* takes place in a Brooklyn rooming-house and involves only five adults and a child. The concentration produces an atmosphere of intensity that helps us accept the characters as personifications of political alternatives in the McCarthy era. The liberal hero, Lovett, whose war-induced amnesia makes him forget his old Socialist sympathies, comes out in the end with a Trotskyite position; though Lovett seems to see, in the Trotskyite McLeod's failure with his wife, the failure of Communism to take sex seriously, to make an erotic appeal to the masses.

The Trotskyism didn't last long, as we see by Mailer's next novel *Deer Park* (1955), where the morally sensitive hero is failed by Eitel, his model of political and artistic integrity, as the hero of *Barbary Shore* is not failed by his Communist model, McLeod. The hero of *Deer Park* drifts in the end into that state of thorough disaffection which Mailer, in his famous essay of the period,

"The White Negro," calls Hip. But the main subject of *Barbary Shore* accounts for the subsequent novels; for the subject—as Norman Podhoretz suggests in his Introduction to the paperback edition—is the effect on modern life of the failure of the Russian revolution to turn into a world revolution. Because the human spirit failed to take the necessary next step in its evolution, it is dying of stagnation.[3] Mailer's vision of general disease and madness becomes ever more comprehensive and strident with each novel.

Although *Barbary Shore* is Mailer's faultiest novel, it is the seedbed of his new style. *Deer Park*, instead, which is almost flawless, is Mailer's lightest novel. In *Deer Park*, Mailer returns to realism, but uses the restriction of scope learned in *Barbary Shore* to give to his satirical depiction of the small Hollywood world a haunting suggestiveness that makes it vaguely applicable to all America. There are, however, two things in *Deer Park* that point toward Mailer's remarkable breakthrough ten years later. One is the development, toward the end, of the pimp Marian Faye, with his illusionless honesty and courage, as a Hip answer to the self-deceptions of the liberal artist, Eitel.[4] Another is the central importance given to sexuality. For the last two novels are organized by a sexual vision so pervasive that characterization is determined by sexual quality and the very fabric of external reality is sexually charged.

The most obvious sign of breakthrough is the new metaphorical prose that begins in *American Dream*, prose that calls attention to itself as it did not in the earlier novels. Here, for example, is the way Rojack, the hero of *American Dream*, describes a German soldier he shot in the war, a soldier whose eyes he cannot forget.

> He had eyes I was to see once later on an autopsy table in a small town in Missouri, eyes belonging to a redneck farmer from a deep road in the Ozarks, eyes of blue, so perfectly blue

and mad they go all the way in deep into celestial vaults of
sky, eyes which go back all the way to God is the way I think
I heard it said once in the South, and I faltered before that
stare, clear as ice in the moonlight. . . . The light was going
out in his eye. It started to collect, to coagulate into the thick
jelly which forms on the pupil of a just dead dog, and he died
then, and fell over.

Here is how Rojack's wife, the beautiful society girl, Deborah
Kelly, looks to him in the morgue after he strangled her, then
pushed her out the window to make it look like suicide. He
caught "a clear view of one green eye staring open, hard as a marble, dead as the dead eye of a fish." Observing the nightclub singer,
Cherry, with whom he falls in love a few hours after the murder,
he sees in her substantial bottom the loving small-town Southern
girl concealed beneath the sophisticated face. Her face he might
possess, but not "her bee-hind . . . no one ever had . . . so all the
difficulty had gone down to her feet, yes the five painted toes
talked of how bad this girl could be." "A sickness came off her,
something broken and dead from the liver, stale, used-up, it
drifted in a pestilence of mood toward my table, sickened me as it
settled in." He retires to the men's room where for the second
time that night he vomits, "and thought that if the murderer were
now loose in me, well, so too was a saint of sorts, a minor saint no
doubt, but free at last to absorb the ills of others and regurgitate
them." [5]

Such somatic characterization, reminiscent of Lawrence, makes
plausible the events of this American dream, in which the submerged or potential becomes manifest. In Bellow's *Herzog*, which
came out a year earlier, the hero wants to kill his wife, but does
not because he cannot reconcile with ordinary reality his momentary insights into her supernatural evil. Mailer's hero can do what
Bellow's cannot, because his insight into Deborah's evil transforms
reality for him. "I had learned to speak," he says, "in a world
which believed in the *New York Times*," but he has lost his "faith

in all of that," because he has learned from Deborah that the forces that matter are magical. "It was horror this edge of madness to lie beside Deborah in a marriage bed and wonder who was responsible for the cloud of foul intent which lifted on the mingling of our breath. Yes, I had come to believe in spirits and demons."

I would call the style of *American Dream* "hallucinated realism," because I want to differentiate it from the ordinary realism that contrasts subjective feeling with the neutrality of the objective world, and because I want at the same time to call attention to its realism. For nocturnal New York is sketched in superbly, as are the various kinds of New York manners. Here, for example, is a bit of dialogue between Steve Rojack and the producer of his TV show, who has telephoned, after the news of Deborah's suicide, to persuade Steve to resign.

> "Steve, *anxiety* is loose here [in the studio] today. It hasn't been so bad since Kennedy stood up to Khrushchev with the missiles. Poor Deborah. I only met her once, but she's a great woman."
> "Yes. W*as*."
> "Steve, you must be in a state of shock."
> "I'm a little rocky, kid."
> "I'll bet. I'll bet. These dependencies we feel on women. When they go, it's like losing your mother."
> If Deborah were not dead, but had merely run off to Europe with another man, Arthur would have said, "It's like losing mother's tit."

The surface is rendered in order that it may be psychologically penetrated, imbued with magic. When the psychological penetration is deepest, the hallucinated realism turns, for those moments only, into allegorical romance.

Through a style that talks with the same words about conscious and unconscious levels of existence, Mailer solves his old problem, going back to *Naked and the Dead*, of the conflict between morality and power. Rojack is the first of Mailer's morally sensitive heroes who can compete with people of power like Deborah and her multimillionaire father. But it is only in the course of the novel that Rojack acquires the strength to compete, because he draws out of himself his own bestiality and thus discovers the source of their power and his. The story tells how Rojack finds his courage and therefore his freedom and humanity.

Rojack, who is professor of something called existential psychology, believes that "the root of neurosis is cowardice rather than brave old Oedipus." By Rojack's criteria, Bellow's Herzog is and remains a coward because he is too nice; he never *does* the unspeakable thing that would teach him what he is capable of. Mailer's story takes place way out beyond the moral experience of the Herzogs, the decent, reasonable people who read the *New York Times.*

That's why it takes place at the top, among *big* people, who are rich, famous, extravagant, who are the equivalent of the kings and princesses of fairy tale. "God and the Devil are very attentive to the people at the summit. I don't know if they stir much in the average man's daily stew, no great sport for spooks, I would suppose, in a ranch house, but do you expect God or the Devil left Lenin or Hitler or Churchill alone? . . . There's nothing but magic at the top."

High on a balcony over Sutton Place, Rojack is at the outset tempted to jump by the Lady Moon, who speaks to him with Deborah's voice, urging him to die. Not yet, he thinks, but he knows this was the moment his death began, "this was the hour when the cells took their leap." [6] The middle-aged Rojack is at Dante's "mezzo del cammin," and starts his descent to Hell.

He starts downward by strangling Deborah in the upstairs bedroom of her duplex, which is suspended over the East River and is hung with a fabric of tropical flowers that provides the sense of New York *chic* and the jungle setting appropriate to their moment of truth. Sexually exhilarated by the murder, Rojack descends a flight to vent his hate in intercourse, involving buggery, with Deborah's German maid. This graphically described bang is a *tour de force*; for it is so thoroughly absorbed in intellectual and moral contemplation that it is transformed—as Coleridge said Shakespeare transformed *Venus and Adonis*—into something other than pornography.[7]

It is only after this further descent into evil that Rojack can reascend to Deborah's room, throw her dead body down to the East River Drive and fabricate the story of suicide. The circle of evil widens at the police station, where we see the criminal mentality of the detectives and learn that one of the cars stopped by Deborah's body contained a Mafia big shot, who has been hauled in with his mistress, Cherry. The Mafia man is released; so finally is Rojack, because of a signal from on high. When the next midnight Rojack ascends the Waldorf Towers to see Deborah's father, he learns who has made the signal. For Kelly is, as he says of himself, " 'a spider. Have strings in everywhere from the Muslims to the *New York Times.*' " He has strings in on the CIA and the Mafia, too. The Mafia man is there; so is the German maid, who turns out to be Kelly's mistress, set to spy on Deborah who had herself indulged in some unspecified political spying. Kelly once had Cherry as mistress, and has even had—this is the climactic revelation of evil—an incestuous passion for Deborah. Kelly has called off the police investigation into the murder, perhaps because he fears exposure, more likely because he has his own plans for Rojack.

As in *Barbary Shore*, the claustrophobic closed circle so intensifies the moral atmosphere as to make allegory believable. The main action is compressed into a nightmarish thirty-two hours; and we come to feel, as all threads wind back to Kelly, that he really is the Devil and that the Devil dwells on top, on top of the power structure. It is God who dwells, if anywhere, on the bottom. That is why when Rojack is on his way to the Waldorf Towers, an inner voice tells him to go to Harlem instead. Although we are not allowed to forget Harlem, Mailer fails to make anything morally substantial of it or of the good girl, Cherry, who comes off as a sentimentalized abstraction.

The Devil comes alive in Kelly because Kelly is magnificently attractive, with his intelligence and forcefulness, and because Rojack smells beneath Kelly's cologned surface something else, some whiff of the "icy rot and iodine in a piece of marine nerve left to bleach on the sand." Because Rojack's apprehension of evil is registered as sensation, we understand how he can *know*, without knowing why, that he must to escape it rush out to the terrace and walk round the parapet thirty stories above the street. This walk round the parapet is the high point of the novel, a triumph of narration. Because we sweat it out with Rojack as wind, rain and psychologically sensed supernatural forces (Deborah's hands, for example) threaten to dislodge him, we believe in the importance of this ordeal, that it is his Purgatory, his penance and way to salvation.

But Rojack does not walk the parapet a second time, as he knows he should for Cherry's sake. Cherry, whom he followed the night before from the police station to her nightclub and her bed, has become his Beatrice, pointing the way to salvation. They experienced with each other their first genuine emotion of love; and it is Cherry who has transformed the Deborah-inspired impulse to jump into the life-enhancing impulse to walk the parapet. Rojack has already had to pass two tests of courage for Cherry—he has had to defy a Mafia thug and fight her Negro ex-lover, Shago Martin. Now, as he rushes off to possess her, hoping he has fulfilled "the iron law of romance: one took the vow to be brave," he is seized with dread. " 'You've gotten off easy,' " he tells himself; and sure enough, he finds Cherry dying, beaten to death by a friend of Shago's. Shago himself has been found beaten to death in Harlem.

Rojack's self-admonition should be answer enough to the reviewers who complained that Rojack does not pay a moral price for the murder. He pays a price in the same way as the Ancient Mariner; and, indeed, Mailer's novel is like Coleridge's poem all about the moral price. The murders in both works are merely the occasions for expressionistic portrayal of the *experience* of guilt, penance and at least partial redemption. The novel, in addition, draws our attention away from the murder to the web of social evil the murder discloses, a web in which Deborah was thoroughly implicated.

In his wartime heroism, Rojack showed a potentiality for courageous action that got squashed in civilian life, where he allowed himself to be used by the Kellys and their like. His marriage went bad because Deborah considered him, and he considered himself, a coward. Now with the murder, an act that disengages him from career and social position, he finds his courage and with it the ability to love. The only really implausible thing in this just plausible novel is the number of Rojack's monumentally long coitions during the night hours that remain after the murder. But this is the American dream—that courage is connected with sexual potency and that a man, when tested, will be found to have infinite supplies of both. The point is that modern American society suppresses the chance of most men to realize this dream by passing— through some traumatic test of courage equivalent to primitive initiation rites—into possession of their manhood. Hence the locked-up seething madness of American life.

In the end, Rojack drifts off to Las Vegas to join "a new breed of men" [8]—presumably a breed recovering the old Wild West virtues by testing their courage at the gambling tables, a breed who if they have not found the good have at least disengaged from the evil. This 'solution' is the Hip equivalent (in "White Negro," Mailer speaks of the Hipster as "a frontiersman in the Wild West of American night life" [9]) of the purgatorial wandering in which the Ancient Mariner is finally suspended.

On his way to Las Vegas, Rojack witnesses the autopsy of the old Missouri farmer through whose blue eyes he has evoked the eyes of the German soldier he shot in the war. The old man died of cancer; and we see here how Mailer's psychosomatic theory about cancer seems valid enough when used for symbolic purposes.

The old man's terrible smell haunts Rojack's nostrils for the rest of the journey, coming back at him from off the landscape like some quintessential atmosphere of America.

> Cancer is the growth of madness denied. In that corpse I saw, madness went down to the blood—leucocytes gorged the liver, the spleen, the enlarged heart and violet-black lungs, dug into the intestines, germinated stench. . . . some of the real madness went into me. The stink of the dead man went along the dry lands of Oklahoma and northern Texas, through the desert bake of New Mexico, Arizona, on into the valleys of the moon—

where sits Las Vegas, described as the volcanic place where the madness erupts.

Does the eruption make Las Vegas beneficial, and has Rojack saved himself from cancer by expressing his madness? There is in Las Vegas another atmosphere and temperature, that of the air-conditioned interiors which seem to contain air brought "through space" from some "pleasure chamber of an encampment on the moon." [10] The moon, which originally symbolized Deborah, seems now to be a good, even a heavenly, thing; for Cherry speaks to him from it, from perhaps (as my colleague Anthony Winner suggests) Dante's lowest circle of Paradise, the lunar circle of nuns who were forced to marry (Cherry conveys regards from Marilyn Monroe). Rojack's madly comic oscillation between the "two atmospheres" (of hell and heaven?) seems to do him good. In the last sentence, he is "something like sane again" as he sets off for the jungles of Guatemala and Yucatán. Why there? His spiritual progress has all along been backward and downward. Hence he feels Harlem is the good place, perceives heaven in the hell of Las Vegas, and sets forth to find what he has earlier called "the beast of mystery" in its jungle habitat. This final chapter is too elliptical to be clear, but the symbolism—moving as it does through smell, somatic imagery, and the unearthly moon, to recall all that was contained in the madly cerulean eyes of the German soldier, who was shot in moonlight—brings to a climax the coherence of vision that accounts for the success of this powerfully imaginative novel.

Why Are We in Vietnam? is even more wildly imaginative in its treatment of the American dream and the American madness. Here the Wild West theme is central, for the characters are all Texans; and though the Texans are satirized, it is clearer than in the earlier book that there is something to be said for the American dream of courage and sexual potency and for the barbaric energies it expresses. In this book, imagination shows itself not in the Gothic nightmare way, but through wit and nature poetry. Narrated by an eighteen-year-old Texas hellraiser, named D.J., the book is, considering its horrendous message, curiously lighthearted and young. One feels in its ease of execution that Mailer has finally broken through, has learned how to speak with one voice about the horror and the glory of, to use his phrase, the American "giant."

The wit is not cerebral; it is the expression of physical exuberance, and employs the word "ass" as an all-purpose intensifier. Mailer has borrowed from Joyce and William Burroughs to create an idiom that is genuine, semi-literate, all-boys-together American, heightened most of the time (sometimes Mailer tries too hard) into wit and poetry. Once you get over the first shock at the unceasing obscenities, they take on (if the book works for you) the quality of metaphor, a way of talking about the whole of life like the somatic images of *American Dream*; and they come to seem the only richly expressive way of talking—the rhythm seems wrong when you leave them out, the expression thin. The obscenities seem necessary for the giant qualities Mailer wants to portray." [11] Mailer has always admired big, strong characters even when they are bastards. In this book, all the major characters are big, strong bastards.

The idiom is D.J.'s; the others do not all or always talk this way, but D.J. shows through the idiom what they are really saying. "If the illusion has been conveyed that my mother, D.J.'s own mother, talks the way you got it here, well little readster, you're sick in your own drool, because my mother is a Southern lady, she's as elegant as an oyster with powder on its ass, she don't talk that way, she just thinks that way." The idiom is also the means of satirizing D.J. and the others. The point of the satire is that these Texas Yahoos, many of them with Indian blood, are living in "this Electrolux Edison world, all programmed out," and are, like D.J.'s daddy, Rusty, who is a big corporation executive, at the center of the non-vital, anti-individualistic, anti-heroic American corporation system. Rusty's God is a G.P.A. or Great Plastic Asshole, excreting "his corporate management of thoughts. I mean that's what you get when you look into Rusty's eyes." [12] The vision is of barbarism equipped with advanced technology.

It is to pit Rusty's God against the vital God of the wilderness, and to pit Rusty against an authentic man like the guide Big Luke, that Mailer sends his Texans to hunt above the Arctic Circle in Alaska. The hunt is being narrated at a Dallas dinner two years later; and to further the satire of our electronic world, D.J. is supposed to be a Disc Jockey broadcasting to the world. He regularly interrupts the action to address us directly in little chapters called Intro Beeps, which are often tiresome. There is entirely too much narrative method for so small a novel; and to confuse us further, Mailer suggests fleetingly that D.J. may himself be a fiction in the brain of a Harlem genius. Mailer cannot get Harlem off his mind.

But the hunt, with its rich recollections of hunts in Hemingway and Faulkner, is the substance of the book and the thing that gives the book its high value. The point of the hunt is explained by Rojack's lecture in *American Dream* on the primitive view of mystery: "In contrast to the civilized view which elevates man above the animals, the primitive had an instinctive belief that he was subservient to the primal pact between the beasts of the jun-

gle and the beast of mystery." [13] The spiritual essence that in
American Dream is suggested through somatic and animal imagery
is evoked here through the rendition of actual animals. The beast
of mystery turns out to be more Devil than God.

We are given murderous little pastorals like this:

> You can tune in on the madness in the air, you now know
> where a pine tree is rotting and festering somewhere out there,
> and red ants are having a war in its muck, and the bear is lis-
> tening to those little ant screams and smelling that rotten old
> pine, and whoong goes his nose into the rot, and he bites and
> swallows red ants, slap, bap, pepper on his tongue, he picking
> up the bite of death in each ant and the taste of fruit in the
> pulp, digging that old rotten tree whose roots tell him where
> we are.

When D.J. feels himself "up tight with the essential animal insan-
ity of things," we see that the social madness of *American Dream*
is now connected with cosmic madness.

Yet there is a difference between the violence of nature and of
these Texans. The Texans violate the wilderness. For Rusty the
hunt is a status symbol, a gambit in the game of corporation politics. The Texans don't so much shoot the animals as shatter them
with overpowered guns. Worst of all, the Texans get Big Luke to
break his professional code by transporting them to the various
hunting grounds in a helicopter.

The animals seem noble just by contrast. Even the grizzly bear,
who epitomizes all the insane force of nature, has when dying a
look in his eyes that makes D.J., who shot him, refrain from finish-
ing him off and step up close to see: "something in that grizzer's
eyes locked into his, a message, fellow, an intelligence of something very fine and very far away." But Rusty finishes the bear off
and later claims possession of the skin, thus disgusting D.J. and
bringing to an end the idyllic episode in which the father and son,
slipping off from the others, discovered love for each other as
hunting companions.

This is the first of two idyllic episodes which are the high points

of the book. Both episodes end in failure. In the second, D.J. and
his best friend, Tex, slip off in disgust at the moral impurity of the
hunting party, and discover for themselves the old Indian purifica-
tion ceremony. Out of the same instinct that makes Rojack walk
the parapet, they advance into the wilderness without any weap-
ons. To protect themselves against a grizzly bear, they climb a
tree, and from there enjoy a panoramic view of nature in all her
subtly anthropomorphized aspects (Mailer's way with animals reminds me of Isak Dinesen's in *Out of Africa*). They see nature as
genial when the bear gorges itself on berries; as terrifying when the
bear rips open a living caribou calf to eat her entrails and then, for
sheer assertion of power, kills her and excretes around her body; as
sorrowful when the caribou mother returns to her dead calf.

> She circles about in a dance, but never takes her nose off as
> if she is going to smell on through to the secret of flesh, as
> if something in the odor of her young dead was there in the
> scent of the conception not ten months ago when some bull
> stud caribou in moonlight or sun illumined the other end of
> the flesh somewhere between timber slide and lightning there
> on the snow, some mystery then recovered now, and woe by
> that mother caribou nuzzled in sorrow from her nose while
> above blue as a colorless sea went on and sun burned on her,
> flies came, last of the flies traveling over the snow and now
> running a shuttle from Baron Bear's pile of bauble to the
> nappy spotty hide of caribou mother, she twitching and jump-
> ing from the sure spite of the sting but not relinquishing her
> nose and the dying odor of her yearling calf and D.J.'s head
> full spun with that for new percipience, since could it be odor
> died last of all when one was dead? and took a separate route.

Even more than in *American Dream*, we are in an intensified
Wordsworthian world where smell and the ability to smell is
an index of spirit; so that D.J. moves, through his question about
odor, into intimations of immortality and divinity. Another index
of spirit is the recurring imagery of electro-magnetism, the suggestion that the far North is spiritual because electro-magnetic, be-

cause it draws up all the "messages" or secret desires of North America. When the two boys go to sleep together that night, the Arctic lights, Aurora Borealis, are out; and "the lights were saying that there was something up here, and it was really here, yeah God was here, and He was real and no man was He, but a beast." The writing here is mawkish, but the point is important; for it is to merge with this great beast of desire that D.J. puts out a hand to touch Tex and make manifest the latent homosexual feeling between them. "They is crazy about each other," we were told earlier. "But fear not, gentle auditor, they is men, real Texas men." [14]

The satire is directed against their suppression of homosexual feeling. Although Mailer has in the past treated homosexuality as a sign of failure, we have here to follow the story, which seems to suggest that the homosexuality ought to be recognized and outgrown.[15] For the same reason that Rusty kills and claims possession of Griz #1, Griz #2 kills and excretes on the caribou calf, so some demonic will to power (there has been a running satire on Texas will power) causes the boys to vie in an unspoken contest for the male role. Instead of love, "murder" breaks out between them and they make a pact in blood to be "killer brothers." The effect of the hunt has been pernicious, as we see by the near-criminal behavior of the boys during the two years following in Dallas. And we learn in the last sentence of the book that they are now off to "Vietnam, hot damn."

Only here are we finally brought round to the irritatingly odd title. Why are we in Vietnam? Because we are crazy and nature is crazy, but nature's fall is apparently caused by ours (the Arctic animals are being driven crazy by the noise of airplanes). And why are we crazier and more dangerous than other nations? Because we are bigger, more energetic, more heroic. The whole book sings our potential heroism, what we might have been and how terribly we have gone wrong. Through joking references to the pioneer days, we are reminded of the old American dream of heroic fulfillment in nature. In the Arctic wilderness, the Texans have a chance to

start over again. They might have found God there; they find instead the Devil, because of a fatal flaw—the need to express their
Faustian pursuit of infinite courage and sexual potency through
the desire to dominate and possess. I think we are to understand
that this flaw goes back to their origins, but has been aggravated
by technology.

"The country had always been wild," says Mailer in *Armies of
the Night*, a book which, in dealing with the 1967 anti-war March
on the Pentagon, incidentally throws light on the last two novels.

> It had always been harsh and hard . . . the fever to travel was
> in the American blood, so said all, but now the fever had left
> the blood, it was in the cells, the cells traveled, and the cells
> were as insane as Grandma with orange hair. The small towns
> were disappearing in the bypasses and the supermarkets and
> the shopping centers. . . . Technology had driven insanity out
> of the wind and out of the attic, and out of all the lost primi-
> tive places: one had to find it now wherever fever, force, and
> machines could come together, in Vegas, at the race track, in
> pro football, race riots for the Negro, suburban orgies—none
> of it was enough—one had to find it in Vietnam; that was
> where the small town had gone to get its kicks.[16]

As an analysis of our political reasons for being in Vietnam, the
passage is no less deficient than the novel that asks this question;
for both attribute the war to popular bloodthirstiness, when there
has never been a war more unpopular. But as a metaphorical vision
of our culture, employing a parable about Vietnam, the passage
has a certain psychological validity—a validity demonstrated by
our unhappy precedence over all other advanced nations in crimes
of violence, and by isolated cases of American atrocities in Vietnam. The psychology is only valid non-statistically, however, and
at a depth that is best portrayed in fiction, where it need not lead
to a doctrinaire position.

Even in his political writings, Mailer cuts through doctrinaire
positions—as in *Miami and the Siege of Chicago*, his account of
the 1968 nominating conventions, where in preferring the coarsely

sensual face of Chicago, represented by its Mayor, to the "thin nostrils" of McCarthy's supporters,[17] he expresses metaphorically his temperamental though not political antipathy to the liberal academics whom he sees as new men, natural managers of technology land. Complexity of political judgment is especially apparent in *Armies*, where Mailer describes himself as a Left Conservative and reveals the aristocratic bias inherent in the paradoxical cluster of ideas we have earlier associated with the word *culture*, ideas best expressed through forms of imaginative literature. Mailer subtitles *Armies: History as a Novel, The Novel as History* to make us read it as imaginative literature. Nevertheless, his political and cultural vision is expressed most profoundly in the novels, especially the last two.

All Mailer's novels are tied to an outstanding event of the time —World War II, the Korean War, the McCarthy investigations, now Vietnam. In spite of his apparently unrealistic new style, Mailer still adheres to the large realistic tradition of the novelist as a chronicler of his time. He remains political and uses his new style to project those unconscious pathological forces that are, as he sees it, the main determinants of political behavior, especially in America now. Mailer's psychological and social intelligence combines in these two novels with a wild, fantastic, unpredictable quality of mind that touches raw nerves in us because it is so alive. We can pick at faults in the novels, but the important point is this—that we sense Mailer's intelligence as a force, passionate and all-pervading, that sees things through to their ultimate causes and consequences; and this marks him as a major talent.

THE
MYSTERIES
OF IDENTITY:
A Theme in Modern Literature

One of the most fashionable literary terms these days is persona—which is the Latin word for the mask that actors used to wear in the Greek and Roman theater. The currency of the term suggests that the identity of the author and his characters, and the distinction between them, has become a problem. When critics call characters in poems and plays and novels personae, they may mean one of two different things. They may mean that the characters are masks through which the author speaks, or they may mean that the characters have nothing to do with the author but are the masks or types necessary in order that the action may be played out. With both meanings of the word persona, the critics are saying that literature is or ought to be impersonal.

Like most technical terminology the word persona is a weapon in a campaign—in this case a campaign against the autobiographical or confessional style of much nineteenth-century literature. It is in nineteenth-century literature that the issue first arises between a personal and an impersonal literature, that it becomes a problem to distinguish between the author and his characters. To

164

understand the twentieth-century reaction, we have therefore to understand why nineteenth-century literature became so personal.

A good working explanation is provided, I think, by the Chicago philosopher George Herbert Mead, in his *Movements of Thought in the Nineteenth Century*. According to Mead, the romanticists found themselves in a world in which public symbols had lost moral authority. Their aim was to re-establish values on an empiric basis. Since they felt analysis could not yield values but could only destroy them, the romanticists developed a projective habit of mind. They came to know the world, not from outside by applying ideas to it, or by passively responding to it, but by playing roles in it—by projecting themselves into nature, the past and other people. In other words, they were aware of themselves as inside, or as having organized, the experience they were perceiving. They thus came to know the object and the self in the object, and it was through maintaining a sense of continuity among the ever-increasing number of their projected selves that they evolved a sense of identity.

Whether nineteenth-century people were as people more projective than their ancestors, I would not venture to say (although the increase of the humanitarian or empathic response would suggest that they were). But Mead's hypothesis does explain certain new forms that appear in romantic literature. It explains a new kind of dramatic nature poem in which a poet, whom we identify as Wordsworth, Shelley or Keats, makes us believe that he is really seeing the landscape or hearing the bird he writes about, and even that he is writing the poem on the spot. The poem is about an experience in which the poet perceives in the landscape "the life of things" which he understands to be his own life, and thus comes out with a larger apprehension of nature and himself. The poem is an episode in his evolution, in his autobiography. We believe in the experience because we know Wordsworth exists, and because the poem is organized not logically—it does not illustrate any idea we have to accept or reject—but psychologically. The movement of thought is by association; all the disparate sensations, memories and associations belong to one perceiver. The psychological organization invites our projection into the poem; we stand where the poet stands, we see what he sees and feel what he feels. The poem, then, is for us what the landscape is for the poet, and should become an episode in our evolution as well. Our relation to the poem is empathic.

It is no accident that the nineteenth century saw the rise of autobiographies in verse and prose and of autobiographical novels. For these forms operate rather like the dramatic lyrics I have described. They derive their validity from their connection with a real person and their unity from the singleness of the protagonist (rather than from the singleness of the action); they describe the evolution of his identity through quite different phases; our relation to him is empathic—we understand and forgive all. There is often much to forgive, since Faust, who sold his soul to the devil and committed many crimes, is a model for the hero of this kind of literature. Faust is justified in the end not because of any conversion, but simply because he has lived energetically and with fidelity to the logic of his own being. He has realized himself completely, and presumably Goethe and the reader realize themselves to one degree or another by playing his role. Literature would seem to have been for the romanticists a part of the role-playing process by which in real life we establish identity. Literature would seem to be most effective in this function the farther it asks us to project. Hence the interest in so much romantic literature in exotic settings, strange points of view, new modes of being—that of children, primitives, idiots, criminals.

To indicate briefly the extent to which all this is new in literature, I will have to oversimplify as though I were making a diagram. In the earlier literature, characters were largely defined by their stations and it was assumed that their actions, their manners and their style of speech would adequately reveal them. This is what is involved in the classical doctrine of decorum—that a king should be given the qualities appropriate to a king and a slave the qualities appropriate to a slave. One contemplates a play built on such principles from the outside, aware that one is not a king or a slave. This is true even of Shakespeare's plays, although they seem in their range of sympathy so far ahead of their time. It is because Lear is kingly that we behold his degradation with awe. If we are not to read Shakespeare as though he were a nineteenth-century romanticist, we must allow our sympathy for his characters to be held in check by plot—by considerations, that is, of their rank and actions. We must remember that Macbeth is, for all his pathos, a usurper and murderer and that Prince Hal must abandon the engaging Falstaff because Hal is destined to be King Henry V.

In the nineteenth century, however, people were no longer willing to take it on faith that the king had the qualities he was supposed to have or the slave the qualities he was supposed to have. They rather suspected the opposite, and what they wanted to get at was the man underneath that crown or those rags, the man with whom they could identify themselves. The real man, the romanticists felt, was not to be got at through his social relations—his actions, his manners—there he was superficial, he was playing a role. The real man was to be got at when he was alone, in nature, when he was "musing"—thinking, that is, by free association—or when he was having visions or dreams. It was not decorum but sincerity that the romanticists valued in literature, and sincerity meant that the author, whether in lyric or in fiction or drama, was projected into the character and that the reader, too, could therefore project himself into the character. In beginning to break down the socially defined outline of character, the romanticists broke down the distinctions among author, reader and character; they broke down the distinction between life and art. The important point is, however, that the romanticists broke down the socially defined outline of character in order to liberate a vital and authentic self the existence of which they firmly believed in.

Now for the reactions against all this. The first, which took

place mainly in poetry, was a reaction against the appearance in
the poem of a person who could be identified as the author or as
an obvious alias for the author. This reaction first found expression
in the dramatic monologue, a form that became important in the
Victorian period and is particularly associated with Browning. It is
here that the concept of persona properly enters modern literary
discussion; for in the dramatic monologue, the poet gives lyric utterance to a character who is identified as completely as possible as
not himself. Yet our relation, and presumably the author's relation, to this speaker is like our relation to the speaker of the romanticists' dramatic lyric.

It was Yeats in the twentieth century who caused us to turn the
concept of persona upon this kind of poetry, when he suggested
that the poet writes most sincerely about himself when he writes
not about what he is but about what he is not—when he writes
about his opposite, his mask. Yet Yeats himself wrote many dramatic lyrics, although they do not always—"Among School Children" is an example—have natural settings. In his *Autobiography*,
Yeats describes a program he laid out for himself—a program that
explains, as we now see, the increasingly personal voice of his poetry as well as the strategy of the dramatic lyric. "We should write
out our own thoughts in as nearly as possible the language we
thought them in, as though in a letter to an intimate friend. We
should not disguise them in any way; for our lives give them force
as the lives of people in plays give force to their words. Personal
utterance, which had almost ceased in English literature [Yeats
was thinking of the Victorian reaction against personal utterance],
could be as fine an escape from rhetoric and abstraction as drama
itself."

When in later years Yeats reread the early attempts at sincere
utterance that grew out of this program, he found "little but romantic convention, unconscious drama. It is so many years before
one can believe enough in what one feels even to know what the

feeling is." [1] The drama had precisely to be conscious; that is what Yeats learned. The only way to avoid self-deception and unconscious insincerity was to turn your life into a play and yourself and your friends into dramatis personae. That is what Yeats did with his friends, with Maud Gonne for example, and what he did with himself and his life, when he dramatized it by moving into an old tower and publishing A Vision, that book of revelation spectacularly transmitted to him through his wife's automatic writing. It is his dramatized life and artfully masked self—his public legend— that Yeats draws upon for his great personal utterances.

Turning Yeats's concept of the mask back upon the poetry of the romanticists, we now see that the Wordsworth, Shelley and Keats who appeared in their poems were themselves personae, and that the autobiographical connection was itself an artistic strategy. It is difficult to know to what extent the so-called real poet is not himself an artistic construction which he himself took over from his poems. The concept of persona does not change, it merely refines, our understanding of the connection between the poem and the process by which the poet, and to a lesser extent the reader, establishes and maintains an identity. We are still in an area where the self is believed in.

The second reaction was against the romantic belief in the self. The novelists took over from the poets the attack on the public definition of character. They came at it from two sides. The realists and later the naturalists came at it from outside to show that public roles were humbug—the banker was a crook, the minister a hypocrite, but the prostitute had a heart of gold. They also suggested that there wasn't much going on inside either—base drives according to the realists, environmental and hereditary conditioning according to the naturalists. The psychological naturalists pushed social role and action offstage, on the assumption that it didn't reveal anything important about character. They analyzed psychological processes down to the stream of consciousness.

At this point the outline of character almost disappears, all characters begin to look much alike, it is difficult to find any positive, authentic core of being that can be called the self.

Joyce's *Ulysses* brings all these destructive tendencies together and shows us the way through them as well. We get the minutely detailed and apparently random and meaningless account of a day in Dublin. The various characters encounter each other casually. The two main characters, Bloom and Dedalus, meet and part. Bloom's wife commits adultery as she has before and as she will again. The characters are portrayed through a stream of consciousness, random, irreverent, full of the basest details. No meaning or value comes from the society, and there is apparently no meaning or value in the events. On the surface, the novel looks like a depiction of utter chaos, both external and internal. But underneath a pattern asserts itself, by way of the principle of unconscious repetition. The characters are differentiated by recurring images and associations in their stream of consciousness, and in these images and associations they recapitulate much of the history of the race. Bloom, the little Jewish advertising salesman, *unconsciously* repeats the movements of Ulysses; Dedalus in his search for a father *unconsciously* repeats the movements of Telemachus; Molly Bloom appears in her final soliloquy as *unconsciously* an enduring earth mother who makes the book's final affirmation.

T. S. Eliot said, in the review of *Ulysses* I have already cited, that Joyce had shown us the way out of modern chaos by using instead of "narrative method" what Eliot called "the mythical method." Eliot uses the same method in *The Waste Land,* where underneath the social chaos and the vacant prattle of the characters, we find the unconscious longing for water, for the renewal symbolized in the ancient vegetation myths described by Frazer. Eliot's characters, too, have unconscious, archetypal identities, and their outlines are fluid; one character merges into another as in a given situation they share an archetypal identity.

The mythical method is best explained by Thomas Mann who,

in *Joseph and His Brothers*, connects it with a concept of identity different from ours. Joseph, Mann tells us, did not distinguish

> clearly between his old mentor [Eliezer] and the original Elie-
> zer, and had the less reason to do so, in that the old man
> himself did not, who in referring to himself as often as not had
> in mind Eliezer the servant of Abraham. . . . The old man's
> ego was not quite clearly demarcated . . . it opened at the
> back, as it were, and overflowed into spheres external to his
> own individuality both in space and time; embodying in his
> own experience events which, remembered and related in the
> clear light of day, ought actually to have been put into the
> third person. But then, just what do we mean by actually? And
> is man's ego a thing imprisoned in itself and sternly shut up
> in its boundaries of flesh and time? Do not many of the ele-
> ments which make it up belong to a world before it and out-
> side of it? The notion that each person is himself and can be
> no other, is that anything more than a convention, which
> arbitrarily leaves out of account all the transitions which bind
> the individual consciousness to the general? [2]

Individuality, which was for the romanticists the one sure thing, is now treated as only a concept and a problematical concept. In attempting to liberate the individual from the social and moral categories that define him, literature somehow dissolved him out of existence. Writers nowadays, who want to face this problem, can, I think, face it in two ways. They can deny the existence of a free and knowable self and—like Beckett, Sarraute and Robbe-Grillet in Paris—take soundings of characters only to make us hear the hollow ring within. Or they can—like Mann, Joyce, Yeats, Eliot, Lawrence—reaffirm the authenticity of the self by finding that in-dividual identity emerges, like smaller Chinese boxes out of larger, from an archetypal identity. "You mustn't look in my novel," wrote Lawrence about *The Rainbow*, "for the old stable *ego*—of the character. There is another *ego*, according to whose action the individual is unrecognizable, and passes through, as it were, allo-tropic states which it needs a deeper sense than any we've been used to exercise, to discover are states of the same single radically unchanged element." When Lawrence says that the "non-human, in humanity, is more interesting to me than the old-fashioned human element—which causes one to conceive a character in a certain moral scheme and make him consistent," he means by non-human, no-conscious and non-individual. "I don't so much care about what the woman *feels*—in the ordinary usage of the word. That presumes an *ego* to feel with. I only care about what the woman *is* . . . as a phenomenon (or as representing some greater, inhuman will)." [3]

This is the point at which we can return to the second meaning of persona—the mask that is required by the mythical pattern, the ritual, the plot—the mask that is there before any person turns up to fill it. This leads to a new conception of how art helps author and reader to establish identity. It offers us masks to put on.

Yeats, in his essay "The Tragic Theatre," tells us that character belongs to comedy and is incompatible with tragedy. "Tragedy," he says, "must always be a drowning and breaking of the dykes that separate man from man." "In mainly tragic art one distinguishes devices to exclude or lessen character." Shakespeare, who gives us character, "is always a writer of tragi-comedy," and it is in his "moments of comedy that character is defined." [4]

In the stories of the Danish writer Isak Dinesen, marionettes and marionette comedies are, instead, the model for this new concept of identity. Marionettes offer a simplified diagram of the double vision that makes art art; for we play along with the pretense that they are not marionettes, that they have purposes of their own, while perfectly aware that someone is pulling the strings. The latter awareness is in the case of marionettes so exaggerated as to make every marionette play a comedy no matter how painful the material. One thinks of Bergson's definition of the comic as "a momentary anesthesia of the heart" that occurs when we see life as mechanical and therefore withdraw our sympathy. Although

Isak Dinesen wrote only one marionette comedy, the marionette comedy helps us understand some of her most distinctive qualities —the deliberate emphasis on artifice and the imposition on painful material of a comic awareness, the awareness that someone is pulling the strings, as an answer to the story's problems.

The movement away from character toward a nonvital, mechanical art is brilliantly charted in "The Marionette Theatre," a dialogue written at the turn of the nineteenth century by the German playwright and fiction writer, Heinrich von Kleist. A famous dancer remarks that "the puppets could be very effective teachers of the dance," because with them choice is at a minimum. "Each puppet," he says, "has a focal point in movement, a center of gravity, and when this center is moved, the limbs follow without any additional handling. After all, the limbs are pendula, echoing automatically the movement of the center."

The aesthetic principle is that the artist does not consciously govern a multitude of details which it would be beyond anyone's capacity to govern. His conscious intention is simple, but if it is aesthetically right, if it is at "the center of gravity," the ramifications will automatically follow. It is the automatism that transforms nature into art.

The dancer admits that the marionette's dance is not entirely mechanical; it is to some degree expressive of the puppeteer. Yet he goes on to speculate that "this last vestige of human spirit can be eliminated from the marionettes; and then their dance would be completely mechanized"—it would be perfect. If an artisan would build him a marionette according to his directions, that marionette could "perform a dance which neither I nor any other capable dancer of this era could duplicate." The marionette would be perfect because the placement of its center of gravity would be, paradoxically, "more true to nature than in the common marionette." The completely mechanical artwork would meet, in other words, the natural ideal; for if the center of gravity were just where it ought to be, then all intentions would be subsumed, the right intention would be built in and there would be no need or possibility for conscious intention to intervene between nature and art. Since the puppeteer could no longer exercise choice, the completely mechanical marionette would never, like human dancers, slip into affectation.

> "Great blunders," he added, "are inevitable. We have eaten from the tree of knowledge; the paradise of Eden is locked up; and the Cherubim is behind us. We must wander about the world and see if, perhaps, we can find an unguarded back door."

Art is the back door to Eden—art that delivers us from self-consciousness through ritual or, in Yeats's phrase, dying into a dance. "We see," says the dancer, "that in the natural world, as the power of reflection darkens and weakens, grace comes forward more radiant, more dominating." Art, however, gives knowledge too, so that it restores

> "a purity that has either no consciousness or consciousness without limit: either the jointed doll or the god."
> "Therefore," I said, a little distracted, "we must eat from the tree of knowledge again and fall back into a state of innocence."
> "By all means," he replied, "that is the last chapter in the history of the world."

We have here the central myth of romantic literature; it is the secularized and psychologized version of the central myth of Christianity—the myth of the fall and redemption. The fall for the romanticists is a fall into self-conscious or analytic perception. All this is in English literature most explicitly set forth by Blake, who takes off from the theological paradox of the Fortunate Fall—the paradox that man, in regaining Eden through moral choice and an awareness of God's grace and love, will have gained a greater Eden than the unconscious state of innocence he lost. In the romantic version, the paradox is interpreted to mean that art recaptures for consciousness the data of unconscious knowledge and thus regains for us our lost unity of perception through an expansion of consciousness. That is the meaning of Kleist's conclusion.

When he suggests in the end that the cure for consciousness is more consciousness, Kleist's dancer uses as an example a concave mirror where "the image vanishes into infinity and appears again close before us." This follows the author's story about a young man who "lost his innocence" because he became aware of his own beauty in a mirror.[5] In Milton's *Paradise Lost*, Eve's first act after she has been created is to gaze longingly at her own reflection in water; and the suggestion is that the fall began at that moment. In Isak Dinesen, there are many scenes in which young women, like so many Eves, first discover their womanhood by falling in love with their own nakedness in a mirror. Her hero in "Roads Round Pisa" (*Seven Gothic Tales*) looks into a mirror to find out who he is (there are similar mirror scenes throughout recent literature). The point of Isak Dinesen's story is that such introspectiveness is analytic and leads to nothing but an endless round of reflection—that the only way to find out who you are is to don a mask, to assume in other words an *ad hoc* self, and step not into raw experience but into "a vein of events," a story. The point is that at the level of experience where events fall into a pattern of their own (the pattern, say, of seeking for a father) they are an objectification of your deepest will, since they make you do things other than you consciously intend; so that in responding like a marionette to the necessities of the story, you actually find out what you really want and who you really are.

The theme symbolized by the mirror—a theme I would call the mysteries of identity—emerges from the romantic interpretation of the fall. Since the romanticists interpreted the fall as a fall in perception, they saw the main problem left by it as a problem of epistemology and psychology. The problem was how to regain a connection with the outside world, how to find a basis for action or an action adequate to one's awareness of one's own potentiality. The question was at what level of behavior—and in literature through what kind of plot—a person manifests his true self.

Isak Dinesen is an important writer because she has understood the tradition behind her and has taken the next step required by that tradition. Like other writers of her generation—Rilke, Kafka, Mann, Joyce, Eliot, Lawrence, Yeats, too, although he is older— she takes off from a sense of individuality developed in the course of the nineteenth century to the point of morbidity, and leads that individuality where it wants to go. She leads it back to a universal principle and a connection with the external world. The universal principle is the unconscious life of man and nature, which, welling up in the human consciousness as myth, is the source of civilization, individual consciousness, and our concept of God's unlimited consciousness. It seems to have been the function of the literary generation born in and around the decade 1875–1885—the generation after that of Nietzsche, Frazer and Freud, the great explorers of myth and the unconscious—to effect a transition from the individual to the archetypal character: from the novel, with its separation of psychological and external data, to the myth which speaks with one voice of both.

Thomas Mann, in the essay I have referred to called "Freud and the Future," speaks of the transition in his own fiction from the psychological and naturalistic *Buddenbrooks* to the mystical *Joseph and His Brothers.* Speaking of the "point at which the psychological interest passes over into the mythical," Mann says: "It is plain to me that when as a novelist I took the step in my subject-matter from the bourgeois and individual to the mythical and typical my personal connection with the [psycho]analytic field passed into its acute stage." The connection lies in the answer, which is "the innermost core of psychoanalytic theory," to "the mystery of the unity of the ego and the world." The answer lies in the perception to which psychoanalysis leads us that "the apparently objective and accidental" is "a matter of the soul's own contriving," that "the giver of all given conditions resides in ourselves." When we remember, Mann explains, all Freud has revealed about "error, the retreat into illness, the psychology of accidents, the self-punishment compulsion," we realize that it is through our deepest desires that we make connection with external events.

The psychological interest passes over into the mythical at that psychological depth where we desire to repeat mythical patterns. Life at its intensest is repetition. Mann tells us that the ego of antiquity became conscious of itself by taking on the identity of a hero or a god and walking in his footsteps.

Mann also helps us understand the comic element in this view of life as repetition. For he describes the characters of his *Joseph* as puppets who know they are puppets reeling off, in the hoaxing of Esau the Red, for example, "a plot abiding from past time and now again present in a jest." The effect is actually, as Mann makes clear, tragicomic; for Mann's characters feel the emotions they know they are representing. The word of Mann's that best describes this quality is "blithe"; for the word implies in Mann's context the triumph over difficulties, the triumph of comedy over tragedy. It is this blitheness—"a blithe skepticism . . . a mistrust that unmasks all the schemes and subterfuges of our own souls"— that Mann sees as Freud's contribution to the art and humanism of the future. The mythical view, says Mann, although it came early in the life of the race, is in the life of the individual "a late and mature" view.[6]

In describing in *Anatomy of Criticism* the mythoi of tragedy and comedy, Northrop Frye tells us that we reconcile ourselves to tragedy, which is the myth of autumn or death, because it leads by implication to comedy, which is the myth of spring or rebirth. If Frye is right, then tragicomedy ought to be the vehicle of the complete or ultimate vision—which may be why Greek tragedy finished with the tragicomedies of Euripides, and why Shakespeare finished by writing those curious last plays that illustrate better than anything else in literature the ripeness or blitheness of which Mann speaks.

One recalls in connection with the last plays Sir Philip Sidney's remark that old writers love the marvelous. One recalls, too, the tragic gaiety that is the hard-won achievement of the aged Yeats in his last poems. I shall conclude by discussing a few poems in

which Yeats both defines and answers questions about identity
that are distinctive of twentieth-century literature.

All through his career, Yeats was concerned with the question of
how you get over from the flesh-and-blood creature to the mythical person who puts forth those magical powers from which all
value and culture derive. In "Easter 1916," he expresses his amazement that the people, whom he knew as quite ordinary flesh-and-
blood people, have now been translated into some other extraordinary sphere of being by their participation in the heroic and tragic
events of the Easter Rebellion. And the point about the Easter
Rebellion is that it was, in the uselessness and excessiveness of its
sacrifice, like a work of art; so that these people have stepped into
a tragic story.

In one of the *Last Poems*, a poem called "Beautiful Lofty
Things," Yeats recalls in the life of certain friends one specific moment in which that person revealed his essence and thus turned
himself, right there in life, into a mythical figure. The poem closes
with:

> Maud Gonne at Howth station waiting a train,
> Pallas Athene in that straight back and arrogant head:
> All the Olympians; a thing never known again.[7]

As applied to real people in real life, the question of identity
comes down to this. Where, among the different aspects we show
to people, and among the metamorphoses we pass through in the
different stages of our life, is our identity? Yeats deals with this
question most completely in "Among School Children," where in
visiting a girls' school he realizes with a shock that the little girls
are staring "in momentary wonder" at "a sixty-year-old smiling
public man"—a man quite different from the man Yeats thinks of
as himself. He feels the great distance between himself and the
girls until he remembers Maud Gonne, the woman he has always

loved, as a young woman, and finally has a vision of her as just such a little girl as these. "Her present image," that of a worn old woman, comes to mind, and his "heart is driven wild" by the thought of the passing stages of her life and his. Where among the metamorphoses is the real person?

Yeats begins his answer by asking a question that contains its own answer. What mother, he asks, would think giving birth worthwhile could she see the "shape upon her lap"—and Yeats uses the word "shape" because he will not commit himself on where the real person is to be found—"With sixty or more winters on its head"? Yeats has now to account for the obvious answer to his question—that mothers do in fact think giving birth worthwhile. He finds his explanation not in philosophical theories about the nature of reality—for theories are as much victims of change as were the philosophers themselves—but in the image. "Both nuns and mothers worship images." The mother worships the flesh-and-blood "shape upon her lap"; the nun, the marble statue of the Holy Infant—because each object refers to the other. The nun's statue can break the heart because it refers to the flesh-and-blood shape; the mother can love the flesh-and-blood shape because she refers it to the marble archetype—she knows, as we all do, that some continuing principle, some single identity, will bind together its various phases. Both nuns and mothers, in other words, worship the same combination of archetype and flesh-and-blood, the same image. But it is also because they worship that each woman can see through the object before her to the combination. It is the combination that makes for affect, transforming babies and statues into "Presences" in just Wordsworth's sense of the word.

The questions with which the poem ends are couched in images that make possible only one answer.

> O chestnut-tree, great-rooted blossomer,
> Are you the leaf, the blossom or the bole?

O body swayed to music, O brightening glance,
How can we know the dancer from the dance?

The chestnut tree exists in all its parts and phases; body and pattern, dancer and dance, can only be known through each other. The images combine nature and art, flux and the fixed idea—reminding us again that an identity is an incarnation, a filling in of an unchanging form with transient life. The whole principle of the form, the stillness, is contained in any phase of the life or movement—provided only that the intensity of the life is made manifest in that particular phase or, what comes to the same thing, that the particular phase is *seen* intensely. The final lines are explained by Yeats's remark in his *Autobiography* about "true Unity of Being, where all the nature murmurs in response if but a single note be touched." [8]

In the poems I have dealt with so far, Yeats moves from the life to the myth. But in two of the *Last Poems*, in "Municipal Gallery Revisited" and "A Bronze Head," he moves from the myth back to the life. In "Municipal Gallery," he sees paintings of his friends and he realizes that they have already passed into the legendary Ireland "the poets have imagined terrible and gay," and that the legend is the essential truth about them and Ireland. In "A Bronze Head," he sees a bronze-painted plaster bust of Maud Gonne in old age, a bust that makes her look mummy-dead and supernatural. The bronze head makes him think back to the vital young girl she once was, and he asks explicitly the question that is only implied in "Among School Children": "Which of her forms has shown her substance right?" The answer is that the mummy-dead head has its effect because it refers us back to the vital young girl; while the vital young girl, Yeats remembers, gave signs already of turning into this supernatural, staring, nonvital head—through her very excess of vitality, through a "wildness" so intensely natural as to seem supernatural.

In "Lapis Lazuli," the greatest of the *Last Poems*, Yeats shows how this idea about identity combines with a principle of repetition to make for the tragicomic attitude—for tragic gaiety. In answer to politically minded women like Maud Gonne, who thought that poets like himself were superficially gay in the face of the pressing dangers of the times, Yeats talks first about the tragic theater. The sum of tragedy does not increase, Yeats says, with the number of people involved in catastrophes. There is no greater amount of tragedy in the world than the tragedy that happens to Hamlet or Lear. It is because the tragic poet knows this, because he collapses all the diverse troubles in the world into the tragedy of a single archetypal figure who walks through the paces of a representative action—an action representing "All men have aimed at, found and lost"—it is for this reason that the actors who play Hamlet and Lear do not, at the end of the play,

> break up their lines to weep.
> They know that Hamlet and Lear are gay;
> Gaiety transfiguring all that dread.

The actors know that Hamlet and Lear are like themselves actors, who are consciously—because the author's consciousness is in them, they are partly at least marionettes at the service of the author's consciousness—repeating the paces of a given action. Hamlet and Lear are, like actors, gay with the aesthetic satisfaction of seeing the whole play at every point of it, and of knowing finally that the action has moved toward its necessary conclusion. The mystery by which gaiety transfigures dread is the mystery not only of art, but of the human mind which in all its endeavors assimilates the disorder and violence of day-to-day existence to its own triumphant patterns.

Yeats makes this clear in the next stanza where he shows the same transfiguring principle of repetition in history itself. Through some deep historical instinct that accounts for the continuity of civilization, we know that "All things fall and are built again," which is why "those that build them again are gay."

Finally, Yeats brings history and art together by reminding us of the blithe wisdom of an ancient civilization like that of China—a wisdom reflected in Chinese art, in the great piece of lapis lazuli carved into the shape of a mountain that the poet has set out to celebrate. The point is that all wisdom and all art aspire to the quality of Chinese wisdom and art as reflected in the carved scene. And the quality of the scene, as the poet brings it to life, is perfectly tragicomic. For though the Chinamen, whom the poet imagines as having progressed up the mountain, stare upon a "tragic scene," and "One asks for mournful melodies," their response is the smiling, comic comprehension that includes and transcends all tragic knowledge:

> Their eyes mid many wrinkles, their eyes,
> Their ancient, glittering eyes, are gay.

Magic and art, says Yeats in his essay "Magic," manifest "the power of many minds to become one." "At whatever risk," he says, we artists "must cry out that imagination is always seeking to remake the world according to the impulses and the patterns in that Great Mind, and that Great Memory." [9] The point is important because tragedy collapses the sort of diverse disasters that are reported in the newspapers into the single disaster that is assimilated to the patterns of the Great Mind and the Great Memory. And it is this transformation that transforms dread into gaiety.

We are back, in other words, to the connection Mann makes between the open-ended ego of antiquity and the tragicomic view of life as repetition. We are also back to what Mann says about the blithe humanism of the future. For it is true that Freud and Jung have, through the concept of the unconscious, connected the mind with external forces—forces that are cultural, biological and even in the end physical. Because of this extension, we are nowadays able to accept truths about our hidden desires and subterfuges that would be unendurable if we had to think of the ego as simply conscious and individual. We are being led back, I think,

to a mood of acceptance like the old tragic fatalism, but an acceptance that, because it will be based on knowledge rather than ignorance, should result not in the fear in which the world was an-
ciently bound, but in confidence.

We have been so absorbed by the negative things our modern
writers have been saying, that we have hardly caught up as yet
with what they have been telling us in a positive way. Our best
writers have not been moaning over the so-called "loss of the self"
—which is really the loss of the inadequate nineteenth-century
idea of the locked-up autonomous, magically potent self that never
could sustain the high claims made for it when it was regarded as
the one remaining source of value in a world where value was no
longer objective. It is perhaps appropriate that the current loss-of-
self writers live in Paris; for they have, in their disillusionment
with the high nineteenth-century claims for the self, fallen back
upon attitudes of the French Enlightenment. Robbe-Grillet gives
us the self as a mechanical recorder of sensations. Sarraute gives us
something like La Rochefoucauld's brilliantly comic reduction of
motives to an automatic pursuit of a nasty, piddling kind of self in
terest. Beckett returns to Descartes' idea of the self as a locked-up
thinking box cut off not only from other selves but from its own
body as well. To avoid phoniness, these writers have, as an ironical
comment on the nineteenth-century ideal, reduced the self to a
mere twitch.

Our best writers, however, are twentieth-century romanticists
who have managed to sustain the potency of the self by joining it
to powerful outside forces—by recognizing, for example, that the
self is not, as the nineteenth-century romanticists tended to think,
opposed to culture, but that the self is a cultural achievement, that
it is as much outside us as inside, and that the self exists outside
us in the form of cultural symbols. In assimilating ourselves, therefore, to these symbols or roles or archetypes, we do not lose the
self but find it. When writers are as deliberate and self-conscious
as this, however, in bridging the gap between the individual and

the culture that seemed to make tragedy impossible, the art they come out with may have or suggest the richness, depth and complexity of tragedy, but it must be in its final effect comic or rather tragicomic. That is why tragicomedy would seem to be the characteristically modern style in literature.

THE TEMPEST
AND
TRAGICOMIC
VISION

The Tempest is probably the last play wholly written by Shakespeare. Generations of readers have for this reason been tempted to see it as a culmination of Shakespeare's vision, to identify Prospero with Shakespeare, and to read the famous speech in which Prospero breaks his magic wand as Shakespeare's farewell to his art. Although critics nowadays hesitate to identify Prospero with Shakespeare, those of us who love *The Tempest* cannot help feeling that it represents a culmination—that Shakespeare could not have written it without the wisdom and technique he had accumulated through writing all his other plays.

We get this impression because the characterizations, for example, are so simple—Prospero is wise, Miranda is pure, Caliban is base, Antonio is wicked. Yet these are not the simple characters of a playwright who cannot do any better. They are the simple characters of the playwright who has already created Hamlet and Macbeth and Lear. And we feel this; we feel we are in touch, through the characters of *The Tempest*, with very real and very powerful forces. Caliban, who speaks one of the most beautiful passages of poetry in the play, is enigmatic enough. But where will you come to an end of understanding Ariel? Ariel's complexity certainly does not lie in his characterization. It lies, you may say, in the poetry he speaks. But that is to beg the question.

It is the deliberate return to naïveté, after the tragic complexity, that makes us feel there is something special about the four plays of Shakespeare's final period. And it is this sense of their special, indeed surpassing, quality of insight that distinguishes our appreciation of the last plays from that of earlier periods,[1] and suggests that we find reflected in them the quality of our own largely tragicomic literature. Certainly, the tragedies are greater, more massive, but the last plays, through their technical waywardness, seem to provide symbolic answers to the insoluble questions posed by the tragedies. We find those answers because of our current interest in myth and symbol, in the undersong or nondiscursive aspects of literary works. Northrop Frye tells us that the structure of Shakespeare's *Pericles* anticipates not only opera, but also "the kind of modern poem where, as in Eliot's *The Waste Land*, the narrative connective tissue is cut out and only the essential scenes are presented. Eliot's debt to *Pericles* is partly recorded in his *Marina*, and some of Eliot's readers have felt that the ideal dramatic form he speaks of so often is better represented by *The Waste Land*, which is close to *Pericles* not only in its fragmentation but in its symbolism of Phoenician sailors, sterile fornication, and deliberate archaizing, than it is by his more conservative stage plays." [2]

The tragicomic quality of the last plays is most apparent in *The Tempest*, because it is the lightest in surface of the four. It is presented to us as a gorgeous bubble, which is blown up for our entertainment like the masque Prospero conjures for Ferdinand and Miranda, and which is just as easily dispelled in the end. Yet *The Tempest* contains the subject matter of tragedy, and it gives us throughout the sense of omniscience, of surveying all life, that we get only at the highest points of illumination in the tragedies. No wonder then that *The Tempest* seems the appropriate statement of age, of the man who having seen it all can teach us that the profoundest statement is the lightest and that life, when we see through it, is gay, is tragicomically gay—that the evil, the violence, the tragedy are all part of a providential design.

The Tempest was probably written during the fall and winter of 1610–1611. It was produced at court in the fall of 1611, and again during the winter of 1612–1613 as part of the festivities that preceded the marriage of the King's daughter Elizabeth to the Elector Palatine. The First Folio probably gives us the play as it was acted at court during the winter. But there is insufficient evidence to support the contention of some scholars that the play was radically revised for the wedding festivities and that the wedding masque in Act IV was inserted in honor of the betrothed couple. Some scholars have even, in their disappointment with the verse of the wedding masque, supposed that the masque was not written by Shakespeare. But Shakespeare always uses a deliberately stilted style for a play within a play; and the masque depends for its effectiveness on spectacle rather than language. Unless new external evidence turns up, there is no reason to look outside the play itself for an explanation of the wedding masque, since the masque fits in subject matter and form into the very texture of The Tempest.

The masque brings to a climax the theme of nature versus art that is central to The Tempest. For Heaven and Earth, Juno and Ceres, unite in the masque to pronounce a blessing on the union of Ferdinand and Miranda, and to connect sexual union with nature's fruitfulness as seen in its ideal aspect. Venus and her son Cupid are, however, as representatives of lawless passion, specifically excluded from the natural force celebrated in the masque. This fits in with Prospero's severe warning to Ferdinand not to "break" Miranda's "virgin knot" before marriage. Nature is celebrated in the masque as a principle of order. And it is shown to be, as a principle of order, inextricably intertwined with art, civilization, idea.

There is good reason to believe that Shakespeare had in mind, and may even have had on his desk, when he wrote The Tempest, the reports that first reached England in September 1610 of the

miraculous deliverance of the crew and passengers of a ship that
had been lost the year before in a terrible tempest off the Bermudas—those stormy islands that Shakespeare refers to in *The Tempest* as "the still-vexed Bermoothes" (I.ii.229). The written accounts of the survivors emphasize the providential quality of their
deliverance, for the castaways were saved by the magically beneficent nature of the island on which they found themselves. These
so-called Bermuda pamphlets [3] go on to see the very storm and shipwreck as providential, since they enabled the castaways to discover
for the benefit of mankind that the islands that mariners had
shunned as inhabited by devils were actually an island paradise.

In exclaiming over the ways of providence, the Bermuda pamphlets offer those paradoxes that are at the heart of the tragicomic
vision—the sort of paradoxes Shakespeare uses in *The Tempest*.
"Though the seas threaten, they are merciful" (v.i.178), says
Ferdinand in the end. And Gonzalo sums up the meaning of the
play through a series of paradoxes. "Was Milan thrust from Milan,
that his issue / Should become kings of Naples?" he asks.

> In one voyage
> Did Claribel her husband find at Tunis,
> And Ferdinand her brother found a wife
> Where he himself was lost; Prospero his dukedom
> In a poor isle; and all of us ourselves
> When no man was his own.   (v.i.205–213) [4]

This is the essential message of tragicomedy—that we lose in order
to recover something greater, that we die in order to be reborn to
a better life. One of the Bermuda pamphlets, *The True Declaration*, speaks paradoxically of "those infortunate (yet fortunate) islands," and even calls the shipwreck and deliverance "this tragical
comedy."

The Bermuda episode must have raised again for Shakespeare
the perennial question that became particularly pertinent after the

discovery of the New World—the question whether nature is not superior to art, and whether man is not nobler in a state of nature than in a state of civilization. It is not surprising that Shakespeare had also in mind, when he wrote *The Tempest*, the essay "Of the Cannibals" in which Montaigne praises the American Indians in terms that helped establish the ideal of the Noble Savage. Gonzalo's description of his ideal commonwealth is a close paraphrase of Montaigne's essay.

The island of *The Tempest* is in the Mediterranean, somewhere between Tunis and Naples; yet it seems more magically remote and unlocated than if it had been given a specific location, even one so far as the Bermudas. By setting his island in the Mediterranean, Shakespeare is able to bring the European tradition to bear on the question of nature versus art. He can assimilate the latest ideas about the New World to traditional ideas of the Golden Age and the Garden of Eden. He can remind us of Aeneas, who lost Troy that he might found Rome. Aeneas was driven by a storm to Carthage (specifically associated here with Tunis), from whence he sailed to Italy. In fulfilling his destiny, he underwent wanderings and ordeals analogous to those of the court party in *The Tempest*, including a banquet involving harpies. It is worth mentioning, in connection with the enigmatic references to "widow Dido" and "widower Aeneas" (ii.i.79–86), that two of the Bermuda pamphlets compare Dido and Aeneas, as colonizers of new territories, to the colonists of the New World. (Dido was the Phoenician princess who founded Carthage.)

Shakespeare addresses himself to the question of nature versus art by ringing all possible changes on the meaning of "nature." Caliban is natural in that he is earthy and earthbound, low, material. But Ariel is just as natural in that he represents the fluid elements of water and air and also those bodiless energies of nature that strike us as "spiritual." Caliban, whose name may derive from "cannibal," is the natural man seen in one aspect. But Miranda is also natural, and the two are contrasted throughout. Both were brought up in a state of nature; and if Miranda never saw a man other than her father, Caliban never saw a woman other than his mother. Caliban is natural in the sense that nature is rudimentary and mindless; he cannot be educated. Miranda is natural in the sense that we take the Golden Age or the Garden of Eden to be our natural condition. She has been superbly educated by Prospero, but education has with her been absorbed in the natural; knowledge has not lost her the Garden.

The case of Caliban is complex, because we cannot be certain that he is human. He was begotten by a devil on the witch Sycorax, and he is spoken of either as something between an animal and a man, or as something between a sea and a land animal. All the ironic changes on the meaning of "nature" can be heard in Trinculo's remark about Caliban: "That a monster should be such a natural!" (III.ii.34–35)—in which "natural" means "idiot." If we take nature to be a principle of order, then the primitive Caliban is a monster, a piece of disorder or deformity.

Trinculo's remark contrasts with Miranda's, when she thinks Ferdinand must be a god, "for nothing natural / I ever saw so noble" (I.ii.418–419). Ferdinand, too, and in the end Alonso think for the same reason that Miranda must be a goddess. Shakespeare would seem to be telling us that your view of the natural depends on your view of the supernatural—on whether you see behind natural phenomena the evil machinations of the witch Sycorax and her devil-god Setebos, or whether you see at work a rational and benevolent providence. He seems to be telling us that every creature can be judged by its potential metamorphoses, by what it is capable of becoming. Miranda sees all the human beings in the play as godlike. But Caliban, who constantly shifts before our eyes between human and animal, fears that he and his drunken co-conspirators will turn into apes or into barnacles, geese believed to be the product of metamorphosis from shellfish.

There is no question as to which view of nature Shakespeare adheres to. He presents here, as in the history plays and the tragedies, a grand vision of order in nature and society; only the emphasis here, far more than in his other plays, is on nature. The fact that Caliban takes the drunken butler, Stephano, for a god is a sign of how high man ranks on the scale of life. It is because we recognize the differences of degree within the human scale that we laugh at Caliban's illusion, but give our poetic faith to the illusion of Ferdinand and Miranda when they take each other for divine. Caliban's crime in conspiring against Prospero is a sin against degree—like the plot of Antonio and Sebastian against Alonso, and Antonio's usurpation of Prospero's throne. Prospero erred in attempting to educate Caliban, just as he erred in allowing Antonio to play the duke in Milan. In both cases, he blurred distinctions of degree and helped create the disorder that followed.

Caliban is evil only when judged by human standards, or when he himself aspires to get above his place. In attempting to be "free," he only exchanges masters; for a slave he is and should be, as he himself recognizes in the end. Ariel, on the other hand, is by nature a free spirit (he seems free enough even in the bondage of which he complains), and he is therefore appropriately freed in the end. There is a connection in Shakespeare's world-view between biological, and social, rank and moral obligation. Thus, Antonio's crime against his brother and sovereign is also spoken of as "unnatural." But Antonio is much worse than Caliban, because much higher up on the scale. For the same reason, Stephano and Trinculo seem even baser than Caliban and even more ridiculous in their aspiration to get above themselves.

With the exception of Antonio, all the characters in the play are saved in the end according to their degree. They undergo a ritual temptation and punishment. Caliban, Stephano and Trinculo are befouled in a horsepond for their temptation to murder Prospero; and when Stephano and Trinculo are tempted to steal the clothes left out for them as bait, all three conspirators are chased away by spirits in the shape of dogs. These punishments are appropriate to the level of their moral life.

The court party are ritualistically tempted and punished by the banquet that disappears when they start to eat of it. Antonio and Sebastian have also been tempted to murder Alonso; and Alonso has been ritualistically punished by the supposed loss of his son and by his brother's temptation to do to him what he helped Antonio do to Prospero. When Ariel, who is invisible to everyone except Prospero, accuses Alonso, Antonio and Sebastian of being "three men of sin," his voice comes to them as an inner voice. Alonso's subsequent attack of conscience comes as a total illumination. He now understands the union of the natural and moral order:

> Methought the billows spoke and told me of it;
> The winds did sing it to me; and the thunder,
>
>   . . .
>
>   did bass my trespass.
> Therefore my son i' th' ooze is bedded.
> (iii.iii.53, 96–100)

Since Ferdinand and Miranda start without guilt, their development is mystical rather than moral. Ferdinand's ordeal prepares him to share with Miranda the vision of heaven on earth that Prospero sets before them in the wedding masque. They themselves appear in a masquelike vision of perfection, when Prospero draws a curtain to reveal them to the court party. Note that Ferdinand repeats in his ordeal the bondage of Caliban. But bondage at the lovers' high level of existence is transformed into freedom and happiness.

Prospero himself is, I think, tempted, when he remembers Caliban's conspiracy against him, to take revenge against the court party; for Caliban's conspiracy reminds him of the conspiracy of Antonio and Alonso. It is inconsistent with Prospero's role of a providence in the play to suppose that he did not from the start plan for events to work out as they do, and that he is actually converted from some original purpose of revenge by Ariel's remark that he would pity the court party were he human. Since Prospero obviously planned the marriage of Ferdinand and Miranda, it is likely that he also planned to be reconciled with Alonso and the others and that Ariel recalls him to his purpose. The point where, at the thought of Caliban, Prospero interrupts the masque, and is shaken by emotion, is the one point where he seems fallible like the other human beings in the play. We seem to be getting, in his lapse from and return to his purpose, the repetition of a moral conversion from thoughts of revenge that took place before the play begins. All the tragic events of Prospero's earlier life are portrayed for us through such repetitions; so that the tragic events appear to us in a comic perspective, since we now see how well everything turned out.

Almost all the characters pair off. As sovereign and father, Prospero pairs off with Alonso; and as magician, he pairs off with Caliban's mother, the witch Sycorax, who practiced black magic on the island as against Prospero's white magic. Ferdinand pairs off with Miranda; Antonio with Sebastian; Stephano with Trinculo; Caliban with Ariel. In his role of providence, Prospero stands alone at the top of the design. Such symmetries are at the heart of comic technique, perhaps because they make us feel we are seeing events from above, as part of a pattern, and can therefore restrain sympathy in the confidence that all is well. The design also explains the sense in which Shakespeare is not realistic in *The Tempest*. He is dealing in simplifications like those of the mathematician. He is giving us a diagram of the order of things.

The play begins with a scene of disorder—a tempest at sea that renders meaningless the usual social order. The sailors are disrespectful to the aristocrats, who in trying to assert authority get in the way of the ship's organization. The good-humored courage of Gonzalo stands out against the irrationality of Antonio and Sebastian, who scream abuse at the sailors—though they are later in the play to think themselves very rational in plotting social disorder.

The storm gives the boatswain a chance to display a natural superiority that has nothing to do with rank.

In the next scene, we learn that the tempest is an illusion created to regenerate the social order—to restore a reformed Prospero to the throne of Milan, and to lead Ferdinand and Miranda to the throne of Naples. Ariel turns the noise and confusion of the tempest into music, the music that leads Ferdinand to Miranda. The play is pervaded, as G. Wilson Knight has shown in *The Shakespearean Tempest*, by the imagery of tempest, sea, natural noise, and music. This imagery sets the play in a world where disorder is seen to be not merely at the service of order, but inextricably intertwined, indeed identical, with order. It requires only a transformation of perception to recognize order in disorder.

It is, I think, because Ariel makes music out of the natural noises of the island that there is an undersong of animal noises behind one of his songs, and the sound of the sea behind another. When Caliban says, "Be not afeard; the isle is full of noises, / Sounds and sweet airs that give delight and hurt not," he catches the world of nature between metamorphoses, between noise and music, sleep and waking.

> Sometimes a thousand twangling instruments
> Will hum about mine ears; and sometime voices
> That, if I then had waked after long sleep,
> Will make me sleep again; and then, in dreaming,
> The clouds methought would open and show riches
> Ready to drop upon me, that, when I waked,
> I cried to dream again.   (iii.ii.140–148)

We say he renders the magical atmosphere of the island. We mean by this that, like Ariel in his songs, Caliban in this lovely speech shows the appearances of things as fluid and ever-changing aspects of a single force—a force that is beneficent, though it may seem in certain aspects evil.

This force is represented by the sea that washes through every nook and cranny of the play, moving the characters to their destiny both by carrying them there and by washing right up into their consciousness. When Prospero tells Miranda of the "sea sorrow" that brought them to the island, he describes the sea as both threatening and loving. We were cast adrift, he says,

> To cry to th' sea that roared to us; to sigh
> To th' winds, whose pity, sighing back again,
> Did us but loving wrong.
>
> (1.ii.170, 149–151)

The supposed drowning of Ferdinand is spoken of in attractive images. And when one of Alonso's courtiers suggests that Ferdinand may have made it to land, he makes us see that, by struggling against the waves, Ferdinand actually rode them to shore as you ride a fiery steed.

> I saw him beat the surges under him
> And ride upon their backs. He trod the water,
> Whose enmity he flung aside, and breasted
> The surge most swol'n that met him. His bold head
> 'Bove the contentious waves he kept, and oared
> Himself with his good arms in lusty stroke
> To th' shore . . .   (II.i.119–125)

The passage—which is, in its complexity of implication and its metrical suppleness, a good example of Shakespeare's late style—turns violence into harmony. It is but a step away from the song in which Ariel makes drowning seem so desirable, because it is, like all aspects of existence in this play, "a sea change / Into something rich and strange" (1.ii.401–402)—into the one force that moves all things. Prospero's magic is a portion of nature's; his providential design is a portion of God's.

Antonio, when he tempts Sebastian to murder the King, uses sea imagery, connecting it with the imagery of sleep and dream to signify the force of Sebastian's real desire. Antonio speaks, through his imagery, truer than he knows; for even his plot is necessary to the providential design of the play. Antonio is an effective villain, because he manipulates real, which is to say magical, forces. Prospero uses the imagery of metamorphosis when he tells Miranda how Antonio so transformed the Milanese court as to make real Antonio's appearance of being duke. The wild sounds of sea and tempest turn for Alonso into rational music that tells him of his crime. And Prospero brings the sea imagery to a climax when he says in the end of the court party,

> Their understanding
> Begins to swell, and the approaching tide
> Will shortly fill the reasonable shore,
> That now lies foul and muddy.
>   (v.i.79–82)

The sea is now identified with rationality.

The most admirable characters are those who can perceive order in disorder, because they have the capacity for wonder. When Ferdinand says "Admired Miranda" (iii.i.37), he is playing on the meaning of her name; he is saying, "O wonderful woman, who is to be wondered at." And when, during the masque, he calls Prospero "So rare a wond'red father" (iv.i.123)—a father possessed of wonders and therefore to be wondered at—it is a sign that he now sees Prospero right. There is an irony in Miranda's famous remark at the end, when she first beholds the court party:

> O, wonder!
> How many goodly creatures are there here!
> How beauteous mankind is! O brave new world
> That has such people in't!   (v.i.181–184)

Nevertheless, it is the whole point of the play to make us feel that Miranda is right—that she, in her innocence, sees all these people as they really are, as through all their metamorphoses they are tending to be.

It is to Caliban's credit that he exhibits a capacity for wonder lacking in Stephano and Trinculo and in Antonio and Sebastian. That is because Caliban is natural. His faults do not stem from a perversion of reason, as do those of the four witty characters who do not exhibit a capacity for wonder. Only Gonzalo combines both wit and wonder. In the first appearance of the court party, we see how differently the same phenomena may strike different people. For only Gonzalo sees that their deliverance was miraculous and that the island is a paradise. To be in the Garden of Eden is, we are to understand, a matter of perception. Antonio and Sebastian are with their witty quibbling—their quibble, for example, over the few miles that separate modern Tunis from ancient Carthage—merely destructive.

The effect of wonder is created in *The Tempest* through a combination of several genres—tragicomedy, pastoral, romance and masque. Antonio's temptation of Sebastian has been compared to the temptation of Macbeth by Lady Macbeth; it is the stuff of tragedy. Our view of it, however, is comic, because we know that Ariel is watching over the scene and has brought it about as part of Prospero's design. The whole action is comic in this sense. The abbreviation of time (*The Tempest* and *The Comedy of Errors* are the only plays in which Shakespeare observes the classical unity of time) enables us to see even Prospero's tragedy in Milan as, in retrospect, for the best. The comic perspective does not, however, make us laugh. It makes us marvel.

Not only the tragedy, but the comedy, too, is dissolved in wonder. Bernard Knox has connected *The Tempest* with Roman comedies about slaves.[5] Nevertheless, Caliban and Ariel are too marvelous to be laughed at as we laugh at the slaves in Roman comedies. Stephano and Trinculo seem a kind of comic relief, just because we do so little laughing at the main action of *The Tempest*. Through Prospero's eyes, *The Tempest* shows us life as God must see it. God could not view life tragically, because He knows that all is for the best. God also knows, as Prospero knows of Ferdinand, that the ordeals He sets for us are for our own good and are not so hard or serious as we think them. Neither, however, could God laugh at us as we laugh at the characters in comedies; for He would not ridicule us, or be dazzled by our wit.

Prospero's view of life is set forth in the famous speech in which

he says, after dispelling the wedding masque, "We are such stuff /
As dreams are made on" (iv.i.156–157). He is, I think, recovering
his perspective in this speech after the relapse into thoughts of
revenge. The speech is, like Miranda's exclamations, an expression
of the marvelous quality of life. Prospero implies, in consoling
Ferdinand for the disappearance of the masque, that if life is as
illusory as the masque, it is also as gorgeously illusory. He implies
also that there is a reality behind life just as there is Prospero behind the masque.

In his detachment from the appearances of life, Prospero regains
an innocence of vision analogous to Miranda's. It is the vision of
pastoral, the genre that deals with man and nature in their unfal-
len state. By swiftly recapitulating all the facts of life, tragicomedy
leads us to see through life with the eyes of Miranda who never
left the Garden. Tragicomedy uses to this end the devices of romance. For romance deals in marvelous events and solves its problems through metamorphoses and recognition scenes—through, in
other words, transformations of perception. When Alonso recognizes Prospero and Ferdinand, both of whom he had thought
dead, he recognizes their magical preciousness and thus really *sees*
them for the first time. The same is true of the crew's response to
the ship, when it is magically restored to them. The recognized
objects are transformed through the transformed eyes of the be-
holders; so that more is restored than has been lost.

The masque, with its emphasis on spectacle and surprise, subor-
dinates all other effects to the effect of wonder. "The fringèd cur-
tains of thine eye advance" (1.ii.409), says Prospero to Miranda
when the spectacle of Ferdinand is about to break upon her. It is as
though a theater curtain were to be raised; as, indeed, it is raised
or drawn when the spectacle of the lovers breaks upon the court
party. All the scenes that offer the characters illumination are
masquelike and illusory. Yet it is through these illusions that the
characters come to understand reality. We all found ourselves, says
Gonzalo in the end, "when no man was his own" (v.i.212–213).

Art is just such an experience of enchantment. The speech in which Prospero breaks his magic wand is not so much Shakespeare's farewell to his art as it is his comment on the relation between art and life. For in breaking his wand and taking himself and the others back to Italy, Prospero seems to be saying that the enchanted island is no abiding place, but rather a place through which we pass in order to renew and strengthen our sense of reality.

In spite of its fantastic elements, *The Tempest*, as F. R. Leavis has pointed out, never confuses but rather clarifies our sense of reality. That is no small part of its achievement—though it is characteristic of our time that Leavis prefers *The Winter's Tale* just because it is less realistic than *The Tempest*.[6] With its bias against realism, and its interest in a symbolic art, our time is better equipped than any time since Shakespeare's to appreciate the last plays. The seventeenth and eighteenth centuries liked best of all Shakespeare's early comedies. The nineteenth century liked the tragedies best, and on the whole we still do. But it may be that the last plays—and especially *The Tempest*, which is as I see it the best of them—will in future have most to say to us. Certainly, the interest in them has in the last generation risen steadily.

NOTES

THE FUNCTION OF CRITICISM ONCE MORE

1. (Princeton, 1957), pp. 352, 354.
2. See the generally unsympathetic account of it in W. K. Wimsatt, Jr., and Cleanth Brooks, *Literary Criticism: A Short History* (New York, 1959), pp. 493–496; and in Vols. III, IV of René Wellek's *History of Modern Criticism: 1750–1950* (New Haven and London, 1965), III, p. xiii and throughout. Yet Wellek recognizes that Pater at his best uses "personal impression" as a first step toward penetrating the "unique quality" of a work and the artist's mentality (IV, p. 383)—both of which Pater treated, I might add, as historically conditioned. T. S. Eliot concludes "The Frontiers of Criticism" (1956) by saying that whereas a generation ago impressionistic criticism was the thing to attack, we have now to guard against its opposite, the purely analytical criticism. We have now to recover, in other words, the best virtues of impressionistic criticism—a recovery under way, I think, in the phenomenological criticism of Georges Poulet and J. Hillis Miller, which seeks to penetrate, through what Miller calls "intersubjectivity," the consciousness, both historical and individual, behind the whole of an author's work (*Disappearance of God*, Cambridge, Mass., 1963, p. vii).

3. *On Poetry and Poets* (New York, 1957), p. 114.
4. *On Poetry and Poets*, pp. 116–117, 124–127.

THE EVOLUTION OF SOUL IN WORDSWORTH'S POETRY

1. Lionel Trilling draws the connection in "Wordsworth and the Rabbis," *Opposing Self* (New York, 1955), pp. 119–120. Keats's letter is to George and Georgiana Keats, 14 February–3 May, 1819, *The Letters of John Keats*, ed. Hyder E. Rollins, 2 vols. (Cambridge, Mass., 1958), I, 102–104. Rollins thinks this passage may have been written when Keats was reading John Locke's *Essay Concerning Human Understanding*, especially Book II, Ch. xxvii, "Of Identity and Diversity."
2. While there is no conclusive documentary, there is abundant circumstantial, evidence that Wordsworth early in his career read Hartley's *Observations on Man* and Locke's *Essay*. But whether Wordsworth imbibed Locke through Hartley, or both through Godwin and Coleridge, he would have been conditioned by Locke's sensationalist psychology as part of what Basil Willey calls the " 'reality-standards' of his time." ("On Wordsworth and the Locke Tradition," *The Seventeenth Century Background*, London, 1950, p. 304.)
3. *Essay*, collated and annotated by A. C. Fraser, 2 vols. (Oxford, 1894), Book II, Ch. xxi, Par. 24.
4. "For thinkers of the seventeenth century, to whom all ideas of development were entirely foreign, the place which is now filled by the conception of evolution was occupied by the idea of composition, with the implied distinction between the simple and the complex. A complex whole being regarded as the mere sum of its constituent parts, these latter were not thought to undergo any modification as the result of their combination; similarly, the whole was supposed to be directly resolvable into its parts without remainder. The whole temporal process containing nothing but different combinations of the same simples, out of which nothing genuinely new could emerge, the historical point of view from which we trace development in time, and seek to comprehend the new determinations which arise in its course, was without significance." (James Gibson, *Locke's The-*

ory of Knowledge and its Historical Relations, Cambridge, 1917, p. 47.)

5. Ed. E. de Selincourt, 2nd ed. revised by H. Darbishire (Oxford, 1959). Other poems from *The Poetical Works of William Wordsworth*, ed. E. de Selincourt and H. Darbishire, 2nd ed., 5 vols. (Oxford, 1952–1959).

6. *Essay*, Book II, Ch. xi, Par. 17.

7. The strongest case for the Locke-Hartley influence is Arthur Beatty's in *William Wordsworth: His Doctrine and Art in Their Historical Relations*, 2nd ed. (Madison, Wis., 1927). Beatty, however, sees Wordsworth only as following, and not also as answering or transcendentalizing, Locke and Hartley.

8. *Wordsworth's Literary Criticism*, ed. Nowell C. Smith (London, 1905), p. 84.

9. *Revaluation* (London, 1936), Ch. v; *Articulate Energy: An Inquiry into the Syntax of English Poetry* (London, 1955), pp. 106–116. Colin Clarke, instead, finds the blurring precisely philosophical (*Romantic Paradox*, London, 1962). Leavis and Davie cite *Prelude* II, 233–254, about the infant at his mother's breast—Leavis preferring the 1850, Davie the 1805, version. Leavis is right. The 1805 version is more abstract and lucid, but the 1850 is more poetical because more blended. After all, the "doctrinal passages of *The Excursion* . . . are," as Leavis observes, "plain enough."

10. *Essay*, Book II, Ch. xxvii, Par. 16; Ch. xxxiii.

11. *Observations on Man*, in Two Parts, 6th ed. corrected and revised (London, 1834), Prop. XIV, Cor. VIII.

12. To Robert Southey, [7 August 1803], *Collected Letters of Samuel Taylor Coleridge*, ed. E. L. Griggs, 4 vols. (Oxford, 1956), II, 961.

13. *Essay*, Book II, Ch. xvii, Par. 6; Ch. xxvii, Par. 14.

14. (New York, 1963), pp. 42–43. See also Christopher Salvesen, *The Landscape of Memory: A Study of Wordsworth's Poetry* (Lincoln, Neb., 1965).

15. See *Excursion* IV. 1264–1266, written at about the same time:

—So build we up the Being that we are;
Thus deeply drinking-in the soul of things
We shall be wise perforce.

16. *The Unmediated Vision* (New Haven, 1954), pp. 33–34.
17. See Geoffrey Hartman's subtle analysis of Wordsworth's sense of place throughout *Wordsworth's Poetry 1787–1814* (New Haven and London, 1964).
18. S. T. Coleridge, *The Complete Works*, ed. W. G. T. Shedd, 7 vols. (New York, 1884), II. Wordsworth's "Reply to Mathetes" in Introduction, Second Section, p. 362 (see also p. 373); General Introduction, Essay v, p. 46.
19. "The primary IMAGINATION," says Coleridge, is "a repetition in the finite mind of the eternal act of creation" (*Biographia Literaria*, ed. J. Shawcross, Oxford, 1965, Ch. xiii, p. 202).

THE VICTORIAN IDEA OF CULTURE

1. (New York, 1951), pp. 57, 73.
2. Quoted in G. M. Young, *Victorian England: Portrait of an Age*, 2nd ed. (New York: Galaxy Books, 1964), p. 87.
3. David P. Calleo traces Coleridge's historicism to the late eighteenth-century Herder—"the first to use the word 'culture' (*Kultur*) in its modern sense"—who "believed that each *Volk* possesses its own individual forms of genius. Who can say, Herder argued, that one culture or one age is better than another?" (*Coleridge and the Idea of the Modern State*, New Haven and London, 1966, p. 51). Herder was anticipated by Vico's little known *Scienza nuova* (1744), which Michelet discovered and began translating in 1824, and which Coleridge began reading in Italian in 1825 ("Vico's Reputation and Influence," in Introduction to *The Autobiography of Giambattista Vico*, trans. M. H. Fisch and T. G. Bergin, Ithaca, N.Y., 1944, pp. 75–79, 83–90). To show the effect of the new historicism, Jacques Barzun compares Voltaire's choice as historian of "four periods of civilization as alone worthy of record" to the German historian Ranke's nineteenth-century dictum "that all periods are immediately before God and equal in His sight" ("Cultural History as a Synthesis," in Fritz Stern, ed., *The Varieties of History*, New York: Meridian Books, 1956, p. 401).
4. "Appeal from the New to the Old Whigs," *Works*, rev. ed., 12 vols. (Boston, 1865–1867), IV, 176.
5. Quoted in Raymond Williams, *Culture and Society* (New York, 1958), p. 62.

6. (London, 1948), p. 107.
7. A Lay Sermon (1817), Works, ed. Shedd, vi, 208–209.
8. In Essays in Criticism, 1865, 2nd ed. (London, 1869).
9. Ed. J. Dover Wilson (Cambridge, 1955), p. 63.
10. (Hamden and London, 1962), pp. 10–12.

THE DYNAMIC UNITY OF *IN MEMORIAM*

1. The Victorian Age in Literature (London, 1913).
2. Hallam Tennyson, Alfred Lord Tennyson: A Memoir, 2 vols. (New York, 1897), i, 298, 302–303.
3. Tennyson: A Modern Portrait (London, 1923), pp. 152–154.
4. Tennyson: Aspects of His Life, Character and Poetry (London, 1925), pp. 296–297.
5. Selected Essays, New Edition (New York, 1950), pp. 290–294.
6. Vol. ii, Eversley Edition of Tennyson's Works, 6 vols., annotated by Tennyson, ed. Hallam Tennyson (New York, 1908).
7. See Eugene R. August, "Tennyson and Teilhard: The Faith of In Memoriam," PMLA 84:2 (March 1969), 217–226.
8. Review of English Studies, 23:91 (July 1947), 244–256. Hough, like J. W. Beach (Concept of Nature in Nineteenth-Century English Poetry, 1936), is uncertain whether Tennyson believed in "the evolution of man from the lower animals" or in "successive separate creations," whether "crowning race" refers to a superior man or a new species. Lyell denied transmutation of species, but Tennyson was an evolutionist long before he read Lyell in 1837. Basil Willey shows how, starting with verses of 1832, Tennyson's poetry implied continuousness in envisioning an evolution from nebulae to earth to man to the recapitulation of biological evolution in the brain of the human foetus (More Nineteenth Century Studies, New York, 1966, p. 83).
9. Aids to Reflection (1825), Works of Coleridge, ed. Shedd, i, 327. Carlyle is quoted in Nicolson, pp. 140–141.
10. The coherence was first established by A. C. Bradley (A Commentary on Tennyson's In Memoriam, 1901), who clarifies the internal chronology of the poem and shows how most of the sections fall into groups. The next big step was taken by Eleanor B. Mattes (In Memoriam: The Way of a Soul, 1951), who, in

working out the probable chronology of composition, shows how
little it has to do with the published arrangement and thus em-
phasizes the artistry of Tennyson's arrangement. More recently,
Jerome Buckley finds a unity that is "stylistic rather than archi-
tectonic," based on "recurrence of . . . imagery," a "pattern of
movement from death to life, from dark to light" (*Tennyson:
The Growth of a Poet*, Cambridge, Mass., 1961, pp. 112, 119).
And I have found suggestive an unpublished seminar paper of
1969 by Frederick J. Dennehy, which sees coherence in the evolution of the poet's perception. Like Bradley, I depart somewhat
from Tennyson's division of the poem as dictated to James
Knowles in 1870–1871, and published by Knowles in *The Nineteenth Century*, xxxiii (January–June 1893), 182. Tennyson did
not, after all, repeat this division in the notes he later prepared
for the *Memoir*, where he makes a simple division based on the
three Christmases (I, 305).

11. Quoted in Buckley, p. 123. "The living soul," read until 1878,
"His living soul." But the line still clearly refers to Hallam, even
though the Eversley note indicates the discomfort of the aged
Tennyson at the apparent deification.

12. R.E.S., 23:91, 256.

13. In *"In Memoriam: The Way of the Poet,"* E. D. H. Johnson
traces through *In Memoriam* Tennyson's developing conception
of his art as an evolution from poetry as release from private sorrow to poetry as mission (*Victorian Studies*, II: 2, December
1958, 139–148).

14. It is a sign of how highly organized *In Memoriam* is that sections
VII and CXIX were apparently written at the same time—between
March 1850, the date of the trial edition where they do not appear, and late May 1850, the publication date. "This is a poem,
not an actual biography," said Tennyson. "It was meant to be
a kind of *Divina Commedia*, ending with happiness." (Christopher Ricks, ed., *The Poems of Tennyson*, London and Harlow,
1969, pp. 870, 970, 859).

15. *Memoir* I, 319, 316–317.

16. All'alta fantasia qui mancò possa;
    ma già volgeva il mio disio e 'l velle,
    sì come rota ch' igualmente è mossa,
    l'amor che move il sole e l'altre stelle.
                                            (XXXIII, 142–145)

BROWNING AND THE QUESTION OF MYTH

1. See W. B. Yeats, "The Philosophy of Shelley's Poetry," *Essays and Introductions* (New York, 1961).
2. The "Essay on Shelley" is quoted from the "Florentine Edition" of Browning's *Works*, ed. Charlotte Porter and Helen A. Clarke (New York, 1898), xii, 299. Browning's verse is quoted from the Centenary Edition of his *Works*, introductions by F. G. Kenyon, 10 vols. (London, 1912).
3. *The Letters of Robert Browning and Elizabeth Barrett Barrett 1845–1846*, ed. Elvan Kintner, 2 vols. (Cambridge, Mass., 1969), 20 March 1845, I, 43.
4. All this has been made abundantly clear by W. C. DeVane in his excellent essay, "Browning and the Spirit of Greece," *Nineteenth-Century Studies*, ed., Herbert Davis et al. (Ithaca, N.Y., 1940), as well as in his *Browning's Parleyings* (New Haven, 1927), and his *Browning Handbook*, 2nd ed. (New York, 1955).
5. *Letters R.B.-E.B.B.*, 13 January 1845, I, 7.
6. See, for example, Kerényi's Prolegomena to C. G. Jung and C. Kerényi, *Essays on a Science of Mythology*, trans. R. F. C. Hull, rev. ed. (New York and Evanston: Harper Torchbooks, 1963).
7. See DeVane, "Browning and the Spirit of Greece," *Nineteenth-Century Studies*, pp. 485–490.
8. *Letters R.B.-E.B.B.*, I, 43.
9. *Letters R.B.-E.B.B.* [7 March 1846], I, 523.
10. Hence Joyce's interest in Vico's cyclical theory of history. In commenting on Vico's cyclical theory, Yeats writes: "though history is too short to change either the idea of progress or the eternal circuit into scientific fact, the eternal circuit may best suit our preoccupation with the soul's salvation, our individualism, our solitude. Besides we love antiquity, and that other idea —progress—the sole religious myth of modern man, is only two hundred years old" (Introduction to "The Words Upon the Window-Pane," *Explorations*, London, 1962, p. 355).
11. Park Honan sees in Browning's pessimism about the possibilities of language a sign that he was experimenting in *Sordello* toward

a new poetic style (*Browning's Characters*, New Haven, 1961, p. 37). J. Hillis Miller sees Browning's language as approximating "whole perceptions," because so "often close to the inarticulate noise which is the source of all words" (*Disappearance of God*, p. 90). This can be true of Browning but, as Miller's examples show, not at his best; it is sometimes true of Hopkins at his best —e.g., "The Windhover."

12. Quoted in W. G. Collingwood, *The Life of John Ruskin* (Boston and New York, 1902), pp. 164–165.

13. *George Chapman* (London, 1875), pp. 16–17. For a detailed analysis of associationism and speed in Browning, see Robert Preyer, "Two Styles in the Verse of Robert Browning," *ELH*, xxxii (March 1965), 62–84.

14. See Blake's poem, "With happiness stretched across the hills," in the letter to Thomas Butts [22 November 1802].

15. *The Statesman's Manual, Works*, ed. Shedd, i, 437. Roma A. King, Jr., derives from the Prometheus passage the title of his latest book on Browning, *The Focusing Artifice* (Athens, Ohio, 1968). See Ch. vii on the *Parleyings*.

16. *Browning's Parleyings*, p. 53.

17. For an elaboration of Browning's argument, see Sir Kenneth Clark, *The Nude: A Study in Ideal Form* (New York, 1956). "The Greeks," Clark concludes, "perfected the nude in order that man might feel like a god, and in a sense this is still its function, for although we no longer suppose that God is like a beautiful man, we still feel close to divinity in those flashes of self-identification when, through our own bodies, we seem to be aware of a universal order" (p. 370).

18. To Dr. F. J. Furnivall, 11 October 1881, *Letters of Robert Browning*, collected by Thomas J. Wise, ed. T. L. Hood (New Haven, 1933), p. 200. Browning's argument would be stronger if he had not confused Darwinian theory with the Lamarckian, which actually does find intelligence in the evolutionary process.

19. *The Marriage of Heaven and Hell*, "Proverbs of Hell."

20. To Lady Elizabeth Pelham, 4 January 1939, *The Letters of W. B. Yeats*, ed. Allan Wade (London, 1954), p. 922.

21. Introduction to Ezra Pound, *Selected Poems* (London, 1935), p. xiii.

22. (Cambridge, Mass., 1937), pp. 365–366.

THE NEW NATURE POETRY

1. Wallace Stevens will be quoted from *The Collected Poems* (New York, 1961).
2. Marianne Moore will be quoted from *Collected Poems* (New York, 1952).
3. "Of the Pathetic Fallacy," *Modern Painters*, Vol. III, Part IV, Ch. XII; in *Complete Works*, 39 vols., ed. E. T. Cook and A. Wedderburn (London, 1903–1912), V, 205–209.
4. Robert Frost will be quoted from *Complete Poems* (New York, 1949).
5. In his excellent *The Poetry of Robert Frost* (New York, 1963), Reuben A. Brower speaks of the dramatic or ironical clash in these two poems between "the social [or realistic] and the visionary voices," a distinction deliberately blurred in Wordsworth. Frost's "integrity," Brower convincingly argues, "is not that of the visionary, but of the ironist," and this makes his poetry twentieth-century: Brower describes the twentieth-century character of "entertaining an illusion in the act of breaking it" (pp. 76–77, 93). True, but the vision or illusion is a kind of 'reality' that Frost manages to keep in abeyance.
6. *The Dimensions of Robert Frost* (New York, 1958), p. 35. In *Connoisseurs of Chaos* (New York, 1965), Denis Donoghue derives Frost's ideas from the Social Darwinism that taught survival as the only relevant value (p. 182). If Donoghue is right, then conviction reinforced temperamental *sabiduría*.
7. Mill's *Autobiography* (New York, 1944), Ch. V, p. 105; Arnold's "Memorial Verses."
8. *The Collected Poems* (New York, 1957).
9. Theodore Roethke will be quoted from *The Collected Poems* (New York, 1966).
10. Vol. I of *The Complete Poems*, collected and edited by V. de Sola Pinto and W. Roberts, 2 vols. (New York, 1964).
11. *Lupercal* (New York and Evanston, 1960); *Wodwo* (New York and Evanston, 1967).
12. It is because, in words of Valéry that express Stevens's thought, " 'The real, in its pure state, stops the heart . . . the universe cannot for one instant endure to be only what it is,' " that we need, according to Stevens, a saving fiction. "Reality, . . .

throughout Stevens, is that which the imagination . . . must
contend with." (Frank Kermode, *Wallace Stevens*, Edinburgh
and London, 1967, pp. 35, 38.) See also Donoghue's illuminating
discussion of Stevens's aestheticism in *Connoisseurs of Chaos*,
Ch. 7.
13. *Ceremony and Other Poems* (New York, 1950).
14. *Collected Poems 1930–1960* (New York, 1960).
15. *Green with Beasts* (New York, 1956).

A NEW LOOK AT E. M. FORSTER

1. (New York, n.d.), pp. 19, 26. For the novels, I am citing the
   American editions now in print—Harcourt, Brace for *Passage to
   India*; Vintage for the others.
2. *Abinger Harvest* (New York, 1936), pp. 5, 8.
3. *Angels*, pp. 112, 136, 137.
4. Interview in *Paris Review*, 1 (Spring 1953), 39–40. Of Jane
   Austen: "I was more ambitious than she was, of course. I tried
   to hitch it [the humor] on to other things." Of Proust: "He
   gave me as much of the modern way as I could take. I couldn't
   read Freud or Jung myself; it had to be filtered to me."
5. *The Cave and the Mountain* (Stanford, 1966), p. 216.
6. *Cave*, pp. 300–304.
7. *Longest Journey* (New York, n.d.), pp. 302–303, 295.
8. *E. M. Forster* (Norfolk, Conn., 1943), p. 124.
9. *Howard's End* (New York, 1954), pp. 24, 22, 187. See Arnold's
   sonnet "To a Friend."
10. *Paris Review*, I, 33.
11. *Cave*, p. 266.
12. *E. M. Forster: The Perils of Humanism* (Princeton, 1962), p. 30.
13. *Goldsworthy Lowes Dickinson* (London, 1934), p. 116.
14. (New York, 1951), p. 71.
15. *Passage* (New York, n.d.), pp. 69, 114, 123–124.
16. *Passage*, pp. 138, 264, 149–150, 76, 78–80.
17. *Passage*, pp. 284–285.
18. *A Vision* (New York, 1961), p. 25.
19. *Passage*, pp. 288, 298, 322.
20. "The Unicorn From the Stars," *Collected Plays*, New Edition
    (New York, 1962), p. 245.
21. *Cave*, p. 303.

MAILER'S NEW STYLE

1. *New York Times Book Review,* September 17, 1967, p. 4. See, for example, Granville Hicks in *Saturday Review,* December 28, 1968, p. 30.
2. Read at Modern Language Association; published in *Commentary,* March 1966, p. 39.
3. (New York: Grosset's Universal Library, 1963), pp. xi–xii.
4. "Mailer has a predilection for last-minute heroes; just as Croft's sudden triumph at the end of *The Naked and the Dead* suggests the changes in feeling that Mailer was experiencing in the course of composing his first novel, so the replacement of Eitel by Faye as the most significant figure in *The Deer Park* indicates the dramatic evolution of Mailer's thought while writing his Hollywood novel. In Marion Faye we discover the distinction Mailer makes between a sexuality which, like that of the movie colony, appears to be free but is really an enslavement, and the sexuality of Hipsterism which expresses a new, radical principle of self-hood. The difference is not one of behavior but of consciousness. Whereas all the other characters in the novel, whether in their political decisions or their sexual conduct, follow the worn paths of consciousness laid out for them by an exhausted civilization, Mailer's incipient Hipster hero has settled the new direction the world must take to save itself: it is the direction of purposeful, as opposed to purposeless, death." (Diana Trilling, "The Moral Radicalism of Norman Mailer," *Claremont Essays,* New York, 1964, p. 192.)
5. (New York, 1965), pp. 5, 76, 100–101.
6. *American Dream,* pp. 36–37, 137–138, 251, 246, 13.
7. Rojack's realization through the intercourse that the maid was a Nazi suggests a significance different from that involved in the same mode of intercourse with the Jewish girl in the story, "The Time of Her Time" (*Advertisements*). I do not find here the homosexual implications the act may have in the story if Denise's accusation is justified. The point here is purely moral, a descent into the depths. Denise's orgasm is life-enhancing. But the maid's ferocious orgasm leads Rojack to see first an image of death and then the redemptive imagery of Las Vegas and moon with which the novel is to close (p. 46).
8. *American Dream,* pp. 237, 217, 203, 269.

9. *Advertisements for Myself* (New York: Signet, 1960), p. 305.
10. *American Dream*, pp. 267–268.
11. "There was no villainy in obscenity for him," says Mailer of himself in *Armies of the Night*, "just . . . his love for America: he had first come to love America when he served in the U.S. Army" and learned that "obscenity was what saved" the common man. "Americans were the first people on earth to live for their humor; . . . so Mailer never felt more like an American than when he was naturally obscene—all the gifts of the American language came out in the happy play of obscenity upon concept, which enabled one to go back to concept again." In *Why Are We in Vietnam?*, he let "his sense of language play on obscenity as freely as it is wished, so discovering that everything he knew about the American language (with its incommensurable resources) went flying in and out of the line of his prose with the happiest beating of wings—it was the first time his style seemed at once very American to him and very literary in the best way" (New York, 1968, pp. 47–48). Mailer is right about the style of *Vietnam* at its best.
12. (New York, 1967), pp. 22, 8, 36–37.
13. *American Dream*, p. 159.
14. *Vietnam*, pp. 54, 70, 146, 193–194, 202.
15. In "The Homosexual Villain" (*Advertisements*), Mailer regrets his unsympathetic treatment of homosexuality in *Deer Park*. But in *Armies*, he rejects easy tolerance of it—saying that guilt is necessary as "the existential edge of sex" and that homosexuality has to be overcome in the process of earning manhood (pp. 24–25).
16. *Armies*, pp. 152–153.
17. (New York: Signet, 1968), pp. 90–91. See also *Armies*, p. 15.

THE MYSTERIES OF IDENTITY

1. (New York, 1938), "Reveries," xxx, p. 91.
2. Trans. H. T. Lowe-Porter (New York, 1934), Ch. ii, pp. 127–128.
3. To Edward Garnett, 5 June 1914, *Collected Letters of D. H. Lawrence*, 2 vols., ed. Harry T. Moore (New York, 1962), i, 281–282.

4. *Essays and Introductions* (New York, 1961), pp. 240–241, 243.
5. Trans. Don Gifford in *Five Essays on Klee*, ed. Merle Armitage (New York, 1950), pp. 63–81.
6. *Essays of Three Decades*, trans. H. T. Lowe-Porter (New York, 1947), pp. 418–428.
7. W. B. Yeats will be quoted from *The Collected Poems* (New York, 1955).
8. "Trembling of the Veil," Book v, ii, p. 300.
9. *Essays*, pp. 36, 52. "There may be in this or that detail painful tragedy, but in the whole work none. I have heard Lady Gregory say, rejecting some play in the modern manner sent to the Abbey Theatre, 'Tragedy must be a joy to the man who dies.' Nor is it any different with lyrics, songs, narrative poems; neither scholars nor the populace have sung or read anything generation after generation because of its pain. The maid of honour whose tragedy they sing must be lifted out of history with timeless pattern, she is one of the four Maries, the rhythm is old and familiar, imagination must dance, must be carried beyond feeling into the aboriginal ice." ("A General Introduction for my Work," *Essays*, p. 523.)

THE TEMPEST AND TRAGICOMIC VISION

1. For surveys of relevant criticism, see Augustus Ralli, *A History of Shakespearian Criticism*, 2 vols. (London, 1932); Frank Kermode's Introduction to his new Arden edition of *The Tempest* (Cambridge, Mass., 1954), pp. lxxxi–lxxxviii; Philip Edwards, "Shakespeare's Romances: 1900–1957," *Shakespeare Survey* (Cambridge, 1958), xi, 1–18.
2. *A Natural Perspective: The Development of Shakespearean Comedy and Romance* (New York and London, 1965), pp. 28–29.
3. Sylvester Jourdain, *A Discovery of the Barmudas, otherwise called the Ile of Divels*, Facsimile edition, ed. J. Q. Adams (New York, 1940). Report of the Virginia Company, *The True Declaration of the estate of the Colonie in Virginia*, reprinted in *Tracts and Other Papers*, collected by Peter Force (Washington, 1844), Vol. iii. William Strachey's long letter, *A true repertory of the wracke, and redemption of Sir Thomas Gates Knight; upon, and from the Ilands of the Bermudas: his comming to Virginia, and the*

estate of that Colonie then, and after, published 1625 in *Purchas His Pilgrimes* (Glasgow and New York, 1906), Vol. xix.

4. Text from my Signet edition of *The Tempest* (New York and London, 1964).

5. "*The Tempest* and the Ancient Comic Tradition," in *English Stage Comedy,* English Institute Essays 1954, ed. W. K. Wimsatt, Jr. (New York, 1955), pp. 52–73.

6. "The Criticism of Shakespeare's Late Plays," *The Common Pursuit* (London, 1952), pp. 179–181.

INDEX

215